J___ 199_

To our _____
Congratu_____ on being
named editor-in-chief
of the terrific
Thinking Reed!
We are tremendously
proud of you and
love you always.

Mama &
Papa

THE

Literary Review

ANTHOLOGY
OF
REAL POETRY

THE

Literary Review

ANTHOLOGY
OF
REAL POETRY

Edited and introduced by
AUBERON WAUGH

ASHFORD, BUCHAN & ENRIGHT
Southampton

First published in 1990 by
Ashford, Buchan & Enright, an imprint of Martins Publishers Ltd,
1 Church Road, Shedfield, Southampton SO3 2HW

British Library Cataloguing in Publication Data

The literary review anthology of real poetry.
1. Waugh, Auberon, *1939–*
821. 008
ISBN 1–85253–234–3

Typeset in 11 on 12 pt Bembo by Words & Spaces, Portsmouth, Hampshire
Printed in Great Britain by Hartnolls Ltd, Bodmin, Cornwall

Contents

Note: the dates shown here refer to the issues of the *Literary Review* in which the poems appeared.

Dear Editor,
                    You are a fool
To institute the petty rule
That puts an arbitrary ban
On verse that doesn't rhyme or scan!
Free verse, in good hands, can be taut,
Elliptical and finely wrought;
Who knows what masterpieces are
Excluded by this foolish bar?
Four hundred pounds a month could be
A prize for *proper* poetry –
Not thrown away on lightweight lines
Like February's Valentines
Tossed off by refugee technicians
From certain other competitions.
I am a double fool, you say,
For thinking thus, and for the way
I follow slavishly that rule
I rail against. Not so! A fool
Is one who, confidently wise,
Knows not where his best interest lies.
We all have flaws – ah, yes indeed!
While yours is folly, mine is greed.

                                        Peter Norman

Introduction

The poems in this anthology are chosen from about five hundred which have appeared in the *Literary Review* under my editorship since April 1986. They were all submitted to the monthly Grand Poetry Competition which I instituted at that time and which has continued, with slightly changed rules, vastly increased prizes and an ever-improving standard of entry, ever since. The basis of it is that the public is invited to submit a poem on a subject set by me each month – it might be the End of a Love Affair, or Poll Tax, or Hopeless Occupations, or Harvest Festival, or the Birth of Twins, or London, or any other subject which seems a good idea at the time. Entries must rhyme, scan and make sense. There is no fee for entry, but the winner of the first prize is expected to be a subscriber to the magazine, although this rule has never yet been applied. Pastiche and parody are not eligible for the first prize, although even this rule has been waived on occasion. First prize is currently £400, second prize £150, with £10 paid to all entries printed. Anything printed in the magazine becomes eligible for this anthology which may be repeated on an annual or biennial basis if all goes well.

My purpose in inaugurating the Grand Poetry Prize, which has received additional funding from a number of individuals and small firms, was two-fold. In the first place, I wanted to get away from the usual run of literary competitions, as they appeared in *Spectator, New Statesman, Listener* and similar publications. Although ingenious, and much enjoyed by the tiny circle of competitors who more or less monopolized them all, they seemed stuck in a rut of clever pastiche and parody. I wanted some serious creative effort from the nation's poets, with genuine emotion behind it, where appropriate, rather than a monthly display of ingenuity and erudition.

My second purpose was inspired by a feeling that English poetry was in a sorry state, by an awareness that my perception was shared by an enormous number of intelligent, literate Britons, and by a hope that the ability and will to write proper or 'real' poetry still survived in the English-speaking world. It seemed and still seems a tremendous shame that our magnificent language and noble verse tradition should be reduced to the self-indulgent jottings – at best silly, at worst meaningless – of whatever coterie found itself in the ascendant in the various centres of state patronage, where the charlatans, the second-raters, the cultural bureaucrats and power-brokers cluster.

To speak of proper or real poetry when what you mean is poetry that rhymes, as well as scanning and making sense, is to invite a certain amount of justified derision. Such a definition not only excludes some of the best poetry in the English language, written in unrhyming pentameters and hexameters; it also includes a certain amount of the post-modern rubbish which relies on broken metre and unaccented rhyme to convey intimations of some ambiguous, allusive or subjective meaning. It also invites tedious arguments about the nature of poetry, seldom put more concisely than by Peter Norman in his elegant poem on foolishness, 'Biting the Hand':

> 'Free verse, in good hands, can be taut,
> Elliptical and finely wrought . . .'

My reasons for the exclusion of blank verse were somewhat arbitrary, dictated by considerations of space as much as by anything else. I do not think blank verse lends itself to good, short, self-sufficient poems, and in order to include a reasonable number of entries I limited the length of each to forty lines. I also wanted the competitors to *work*. Blank verse is too easy, once you get into the swing of it, and if we were going to have to read the stuff, I wanted to be sure that some effort had gone into its composition.

However, my reasons for excluding free verse, however taut, elliptical and finely wrought, were basic to the inspiration of the enterprise. By the beginning of 1986, when I left *Private Eye* to take up my duties as Editor of the *Literary Review*, it was painfully apparent to anyone outside the universities, the English literature departments and the hectic little world of patronage panels and Arts Council scroungers, that the modern movement in poetry at least, if not in all the other arts, had run out of steam some forty years earlier. It had lost even what little vitality could be wrung from a sincere desire to *épater les bourgeois*, since most of the literate bourgeoisie had jumped on the bandwagon which Dr Leavis led. We all remember, no doubt, the excitement with which we first discovered Eliot at the age of fifteen or sixteen, the pride with which we identified his most obscure references, the sense of belonging to an intellectual and cultural elite which appreciation of Eliot somehow encouraged.

Twenty-eight years after *The Waste Land*, Eliot's three dismally accessible 'comedies', starting with *The Cocktail Party* (1950), might have warned us that his was not the greatest intellect of our time; while the sensational mediocrity of his imitators, like Christopher Fry, should have warned us that whatever touch of genius might be discernible in Eliot, his work did not provide a useful model for anyone else.

To assert at this late stage that Eliot is a tremendously over-rated poet would be as otiose as it would be tendentious. But it has become painfully apparent that the modern movement in poetry, however exciting it was at the time, must now be seen as a picturesque cul-de-sac of English letters. Its preoccupations were neither sublime nor enduring, and its talents were limited. Its imitators, lacking even that innovative spark, are a disgrace to English literature.

When I became Editor of the *Literary Review* I had the assistance of a Poetry Editor in Carol Rumens, a highly regarded poet in her own right, and possessed of a patience and compassion in dealing with other poets to which I could not aspire. After an incident in which we found ourselves with a hole in the magazine on press day and filled it with eight inches of gibberish masquerading as a poem, written in twenty minutes flat by the editorial assistant, Mr Grub Smith – nobody noticed the difference – I decided to print no more 'modern poetry' in the magazine, and Carol left in a state of understandable dudgeon. I then discovered what her patience and nobility of spirit had concealed, that we were receiving anything up to ten pounds' weight of 'modern poetry' a week. Simply to have read it would have taken up all my time – let alone trying to separate the wheat from the chaff, to puzzle out the deeply significant from the meaningless.

In the end, I decided that the time had come to return to basics. If the continuing *Literary Review* Grand Poetry Competition, and this anthology, can encourage the British to read poetry again – as well as write it – I will die a happy man.

The final selection, from poems chosen by the *Literary Review* panel, has been by Toby Buchan. He has done all the work, and it is to him that thanks and congratulations are due.

Auberon Waugh, August 1990

Birthday Odes

Anna Harley Durie: On the Anniversary of Her Birth

I think of you as I watch the pout-lipped
Youngsters on the train,
Their curved, chipmunk cheeks stuffed with self-regard.
I think of you again
When grey women, weighed down with shopping, climb
On, tilting worn faces.
Children, then, and baffled women on trains,
To all kinds of places,
Bring you back in a rush of too-late love
From a cheeky young fool
Grown to run-of-the-mill, middle-aged regret
That youth is cruel.
I carry your bags from the wet platform,
Order up tea,
Pour it kindly, crack a joke and bask
As you smile at me,
Quite simply, without rancour, through the steam.
Two at table. Flashback. Rewrite. Dream.

Elspeth Durie

Gardener's Birthday

'Eighty. It's time to retire!'
I look at your face, realise
How it maps each toiling year,
How shadows on cheeks and eyes
Show the evening is here,
As your sun goes down like fire.

Like fire your spirits flare;
A lifetime of open air
Draws up your gardener's pride
And lights the love that's there.
'Will you sit by your chimneyside,'
I ask, 'in your favourite chair?'

'Sit? I've a bit to do!'
The manner you say it sings
Your courage; I echo an ode
To your scrupulous world of things,
Not in the classical mode,
But the way that's straight, like you.

Paul Griffin

A Pendant Heart

For you I'll buy some trinket bright as gold,
So you can hang my ornamental heart
Around your neck, and let your breasts enfold
    Its purchased art.

And yet you'll find my gift equivocal
At best. A somewhat overstated show
From someone turned a pest. A necklace grown
    Umbilical.

My hope suspends upon a pendant heart
To charm some reassessment of my case.
But yet I fear embarrassment, and start
    To look abased.

Still I shall buy this gleam of gold for you,
And send it with embellishment, an ode.
No words of mine can change your heart. They're code,
    And have no clue.

K. Lloyd-Thompson

Elegies

An Elegy for Miss Ratcliffe

You are the perfect ghost, and understand
The quiet rituals of your return.
You sit with me sometimes, and in the dusk,
Opals burn cloudy fires on your hand.

You were at home in rooms designed for tea:
Translucent china, fields of Axminster.
I made lovers for you in my head,
Killed in the War, poor things, or lost at sea.

You spoke of Laocoon: I saw it all –
The limbs contorted on the beach at Troy
Were visible just where the blackboard was,
And serpent's scales silvered the classroom wall.

Drawing the curtains closed, I feel your shade
Approving birds and sprays of peonies.
Your hand is on your hair, patting the bun,
Checking the complications of the braid.

Adèle Geras

The rainclouds group in the west
And swallows sit in a row
Numbering-off as they rest
Bracing themselves to go.

But you are already gone
Though nobody quite knows where.
The last bus is trundling on
With always a seat to spare.

The carpet rucks in the hall,
The aerial taps at the eaves,
Nothing here changes at all.
Grief is for he who grieves.

It's too late to suffer for you
And selfish to suffer for me,
But I do and I do and I do
Though I pray you are happy and free.

J. C. M. Hepple

June, Wine and Roses

A June of wine and roses,
A girl in apple green
Was all my thought of heaven
When I was seventeen.

But love was drowned in downpour
And broken in the breeze;
The roses wilt on Bredon
And the wine has bitter lees.

Sheila Sullivan

The bees are drunk on borage,
And beetles sip the dew
In open-hearted roses,
And I would drink of you.

But our November bodies
Grow sere, and senses shrink,
And tremble at June's nectar
And seldom dare to drink.

Pat Buik

If June could last till Christmas
And flowers never died
We'd spend December lying
In meadows, side by side;

But Summer will be over
Before it's half begun,
And we'll crawl back to London
To share the noisy fun

Of offices and parties,
Pub plonk and cold meat-pies –
June's long run-up to Christmas
For squalid adman's lies.

R. V. Smith

Hymns to Idleness

Come Judgement Day, when nothing may be hid,
Someone will ask me what on Earth I did.
Seven deadly sins — just one I must confess
For my besetting sin was Idleness.

Envy I sought not, nor to be admired,
I would go hungry rather than be tired;
Richly untilled I leave this mortal soil,
Free for all fellows who rejoice in toil.

I meet my doom without too much alarm,
Who did no good but very little harm;
Up with the Angels, down where Devils lurk,
I shall be happy if I need not work.

Sleeping or waking, innocent and pure,
Clasped to thy bosom, finally secure,
Let me forever know thy soft caress,
Mother and sister, blessed Idleness!

Richard Dobson

Come, rest with me and watch the lazy tide.
Don't wriggle, though — that's what I can't abide.
Someone who hops and fidgets like a flea
Is no companion for a sloth like me.

O what a perfect way to spend each day,
Blowing the dandelion clocks away,
Watching the sun caress the sleepy sea —
This is the life that says it all to me.

Watching the grass grow, hour by gentle hour,
Watching each daisy bud become a flower.
Hedonists now and always we shall be –
Pass the champagne. Please open it for me.

Singing's too tiring, though I must confess
I sometimes hum a Hymn to Idleness.
Music's demanding – and symphony
Drains all the energy and life from me.

Breathe deeply in, and out, and close your eyes.
Doze in the sunshine pouring from the skies.
Peace and inertia all around I see –
Blest are the idle. O, come rest with me.

Pamela Holden

'Go to the ant,' the zealous preacher cried.
I did; which led me shortly to decide
That, rather than submit my life to that,
I'd take as model the domestic cat.

Observe its ways. It comes and goes at ease,
Does not assert itself or seek to please,
And, softened by the comforts of the house,
Is powerless to hurt the smallest mouse.

In aspiration lies all discontent.
Then let us, like the cat, be indolent
Until, by provident inaction, we
No longer seek to do, but learn to be.

Noel Petty

A Christmas Card

Christmas Sonnet

Can cows commit a crime or stare with pride
From dark soft bovine eyes into the mind
Of God? Do dogs howl out, or grind
Their teeth, and snarling, drooling, so deride
Their Maker? – Or a long-haired cat compose
Her lovely limbs, and neatly curl her tail,
Then look upon the King of Kings, and rail
At Him for making her? Do you suppose
That cowshed was a clinic? Angels cleared
The floor of fleeing mice, and chasing cats,
And itching dogs? But their humility
Shone round the messy stable where they reared
Their young upon the straw. They sat on mats
To contemplate their God in purity?

Ben Ruthven

A Christmas Card

Some have no use for Scrooge's goose
But to prolong its span:
Geese assert the rights of geese
And men the rights of man.

Some despise the mincemeat pies,
The pudding makes them ill,
And so does the theology
Of Cecil B. de Mille.

Some would pray to St Gênet
Or bow down to Buñuel –
Intolerant of Limbo,
They finish up in Hell.

High-criticism of cards and crackers
We need not defend:
Priggish, po-faced disbeliefs
Are easy to suspend.

John Hems

New Year

The year sweeps in like sudden fog
Upon a dirty road;
One happens on it as a dog
Might come across a toad.

Confront it, then: its greenery
Behind which bigots kneel,
And choose its tercentenary
With missionary zeal.

The revolution's Glorious
You wish to celebrate?
One shouldn't be censorious?
Hang bunting from the gate?

All history a New Year twists
To suit its smiling face:
The Protestant puts on his fists,
The Catholic packs his case.

Parades; the polished feet; the beat
Of stick upon a drum;
The silhouettes of time repeat
King William is come.

The New Year, then: a barricade
Your town-hall type erects
Is ready for its serenade,
Collision of the sects.

Yet while the sky is overcast,
Might one peruse this fact?
In *Eighteen*-eighty-eight, there passed
The County Councils Act.

Bill Greenwell

The calendar's last sheet is torn away,
Symbolic of an end. One might expect
The sky to crack in two at break of day
Or some old star to die, and so bisect
Time's regulated passage, but the grey

Of January's dawn seems much the same
As that of any winter month, the birds
Are just as dumb, the shallow yellow flame
That licks our sky's perimeter still girds
The same old global grief, as if a game

Unfinished from the night before went on.
In spite of this we humans must invent
A way to make new starts, past errors gone
Or put behind, without embitterment.
And so you dawn, New Year, your halcyon

Wing feathers elevating us above
All daily irritations and disputes,
With promises of friendship, even love,
With resolution striking at the roots
Of human fallibility, the dove

Imbued with claws of steel and heart of fire.
As year rolls into year the same exchange
Of greetings is intoned, the same desire
For better things expressed, as if the range
Of human thought were caught within a tyre

Around the annual wheel, no breaks or seams
But patterned in its seasons. We repeat
The usual good wishes, voice our dreams
In faith to make the past, the old complete,
The future unimpaired by faulty schemes

And deep embedded habits. So we say
Good health, good luck, and may this be the year
When everything goes right in work and play.
Our hope transcends experience and fear
As New Year tears the old year's flaws away.

Katie Mallett

Dereliction

The winters are the worst. No, not the cold
And wind, we cope with them all right.
The archway shelters us, and if you fold
Some newspapers inside your clothes at night
It's really not too bad. The dampness, too:
Although I used to notice it at first,
You'd marvel what a cardboard box can do.
But all the same, the winters are the worst.

Sometimes in summer people stop and stare,
Or wander in the streets at human pace,
And at such times I almost feel I share
A common ancestry with this strange race.
But when, in early winter dusks, I turn
And linger at the entrance of the station
As alien as a boulder in a burn
Surrounded by a tide of destination;
Or when, in tower blocks across the water,
The office lights in random clusters spread
Like multiplying cells in brick and mortar,
Each with its bowed and reverential head
Intent on keyboard, telephone or screen,
I feel again like Adam, newly cursed.
What is it all about? What does it mean?
God bless you, sir. The winters are the worst.

Noel Petty

A broken heart's not terminal, you said,
To ease your conscience for the tears I shed:
You may be right, but if I am not dead
Please tell me who this corpse is in my bed.

Richenda Miers

Once there were saplings in the upper wood;
They gave a stately music to the day,
By any listener simply understood –
Green branches singing in an ordered way.
But now the gusts and whistles of the gale
Have turned about their message and their state
Into a complex webbing that I fail
To understand, that leaves me desolate.
These saplings bending to the weather's force
Have grown and broken to a savage wood
Whose unfamiliar rhythm and discourse
Cannot by human ears be understood;
And only power beyond my power to rouse
Can find the music in these windy boughs.

Paul Griffin

The children built their castle keep
Where sand and slimy rocks converge.
They nursed an old destructive urge
To watch the cold grey water seep
Around the battlements and creep
Higher and higher till one surge
Should mount the fastness and submerge
Their work, but tides were at the neap.
Next morning when the boys returned
A matchstick flag still flew above
The stalwart tower that they had built,
It was as though the sea had spurned
Their labour sacrifice, of love,
And would not take it back for silt.

Ginger Jelinek

Madness

Lips that twitter, palsied hands,
Rather too-apparent tics,
Language no one understands,
Feet which offer idle kicks —

Hatters, tattered, dressed in spats,
Scraping nails on whitewashed walls,
Ducking as if buzzed by bats,
Letting out indecent calls —

Corpulent, or matchstick-thin,
Lemur eyes half-full of tears,
Sobbing in a silent din,
Showing off some friendly leers —

Bedlamites in dirty robes,
Tied by ankle, wrist and head,
Stoical, so many Jobs,
Or banging heaving breasts instead —

Inconoclasts with patchy hair,
Pillar-perchers, batty scribes,
All the fun of every fair,
Harmless victims of loose jibes —

Brains askew and logic gone,
These, we think, are lunatics,
People we should ponder on —
What proportion? 'One in six'?

But actually, the madmen roam
In modest garb along your street,
Tip their hats, and saunter home,
Never raise their voice in heat,

Sit by day in shuttered rooms,
Compiling files and counting stock;
When the Day of Judgement comes,
They will stop to watch the clock.

Indeed, these mental cases stitch
The fabric of our duller days:
We're the ones who foam and twitch
Beneath their pleasant, passive gaze.

Bill Greenwell

Madness

Firstly he lost the power to sleep
Then found it hard to keep from tears
When people spoke to him; odd fears
Began occurring – he could keep
Explaining in a lucid way
Why he was feeling tired and low,
But what he really didn't know
Was how to calm his deep dismay.

The useless action of his brain
Accelerated faster, faster,
He sensed an imminent disaster
But couldn't slow the hurtling train
Of argument that tried to scotch
The terrors popping up all round.
As soon as one was stalled he found
Another kicked him in the crotch.

Time isn't always quick to heal.
In lucid intervals he brooded
On past shames – nothing was excluded –
But presently he ceased to feel,
And raging, unremitting thought
Filled his horizon; senseless chains
Of words; he tried to slit his veins.
Eh bien! They locked him up of course.

Ginger Jelinek

Succulent

Beside my bed's a squat
Tongue-tree, all pimpled green
And barky brown. It's not
A pretty sight. Obscene,

It squats there dustily
Sucking my sap by stealth;
Outsiders cannot see
Its monstrous state of health.

I have a razorblade
Beneath my pillow. See?
I mustn't be afraid:
It's either it or me.

Peter Norman

The Madman

He lived along our street. He'd often stand
Beside his gate, just watching, goggled-eyed,
And if he spoke we could not understand
His mumbled garbled words. We knew inside
His shabby house he kept a mewling host
Of tattered tabby cats that made it stink.
Some said he was possessed. Some said a ghost
Had sent him lunatic, and so we'd shrink
Away from him in fear. If we passed by
It was across the road, at running pace.
As children we were certain we would die
If we should stop and look him in the face.
I see him now, his cheek a running sore,
A soldier shot and shellshocked from the war.

Katie Mallett

April Fools

When alcohol removes the need
For honesty and taste
The naked ape prepares to breed
Or else to go to waste.
Whichever course, a marriage bed
Exacerbates the fun:
A rag, a bone, a lump of lead –
And it is quickly done.

You know her well, from craven youth,
The woman of your drinks,
Who *in flagrante* tells the truth
And *in extremis* thinks;
Whose breast you beat in semaphore
And cover when it sags;
Whose shaven hooves you kneel before
When conversation flags.

Mascara'd in da Vinci's paint
Or grinning from page three:
Contessa, peasant, mother, saint,
Hard left or SDP –
No difference of rank lets Eve
Deflect her from her cause:
To come and, having come, receive
Her own polite applause.

If perjury be done and said
There's plenty more to tell:
Of joint accounts in legal aid
And single fares to hell;
Of reason tossed like salad and
Of cheques forever blank.
For this you have your tiny gland
To answer for and thank.

It takes a moment's ecstasy
To satisfy a wife
But only infidelity
Will make her yours for life.
Of all the tortures that secure
The triumph of the West
The rack may have the most allure
But charity is best.

So let us drink to folly and
The flesh on which it eats.
For no man is an island
Except between the sheets.
And don't forget the sequel –
Women's only rule of thumb:
That every man is equal
In the depths that he will plumb
Beforehand.

Sean Regan

In former days we indicated fools
As those who fished the moon from summer's pools.
Their hats were conical. They sat on stools.

Or capered at the call of fife or drum.
The worst that you could say of them was 'dumb'.
Their holiness was recognised by some.

But nowadays an educated breed
Shakes bells and bladders, tells us what to read
And feel, and how to fuck and how to feed

As if we were the fools: Well, may be so
How eagerly we flock their medicine show
Exchanging something high for something low.

Ignis fatuus, still we chase its light
Through strawberry fields by muddy moonless night
All suckers – maybe Dukinfield was right.

Jim Smith

Weep, fool, weep,
And so let fall
The wet pool of your verse
To seep across the page
Like some perverse
Inverted Rorschach blot,
Which plots its outline
From your thought
And not,
As is the normal case,
The other way about.

Simon Holt

When lovely woman stoops to folly
With another woman's man,
She sits in bed the morning after
Wondering how it all began.

Too late for her to seek escape now:
Wheels are turning, deeds are done;
When lovely woman stoops to folly,
Lies and tears are just begun.

Virginia Rounding

Hopeless Occupations

Of Silent Nights

The Sunday bells peal out their hymn
But locked inside his holy cell
The priest beholds no seraphim,
But alcoholic shades of hell.
His empty pews, he knows full well,
Are God's reply for forty years
Of penitential doubts and fears.

His lips alone believe the prayer
That daily mocks his hopeless heart,
Nor can he shed his cruel despair
On those who do not know the part
He plays for God; he has the art
Of healing souls that vice was won,
And yet he cannot heal his own.

A cardinal could learn to cope –
He has the wealth to compensate,
But priestly vows are void of hope,
With nothing much to celibate;
His calendar becomes his fate
With climaxes around each feast.
Who is more hopeless than a priest?

For each and every word he speaks
Is worthless as a brain in Brent,
He spends his evenings counting weeks
To Pentecost, or after Lent.
He wonders why the hell he went
To study stuff he cannot use.
Depression lives in empty pews.

To fill his hours he starts a choir,
To add some purpose to his day,
But cynics claim that his desire
Is earthlier, that he is gay.
No matter what, they turn away,
His enterprises always lose:
Thus does our priest find faith in booze.

Frank McDonald

Sisyphus Looks Down Into the Valley

I push my boulder up the mountain side,
A job in which I take a modest pride.
The slope affords me a disturbing view
Of all the things that other people do
To help them fill the minutes of the day.
That man's a local radio DJ.
Look! Here's a pop star! There's a chat show host!
I can't decide which one I pity most.
I see them getting rich and growing fat,
Purveying raucous sounds and mindless chat.
They must be guilty of some dreadful crime
To be condemned to such a waste of time.
Oh! Now I see a gang of soccer fans
Constrained to go on guzzling out of cans
Some liquid brewed to stupefy the brain,
Until the stomach casts it up again.
They try to sing but only prove they can't
With their discordant trisyllabic chant.
These youths are permanently unemployed,
Their lives of purpose and of hope devoid.
I turn away, my senses numb with shock,
And thank the gods for giving me this rock.

Keith Norman

22

Hopeless Occupations

Your public executioner has little thought of glory:
It isn't till he's sixty that the papers buy his story.
Until this rest from setting traps or even wielding axes,
It's just a neck or two to crack. There's nothing much that taxes.
The hood is free, the hours short (if totally unsocial),
But who expects that anyone dispensing dread or woe shall
Hobble home at daybreak, flush with compliments from coppers?
There's not a band of boys as bleak as honorary toppers.

Imagine, if you will, the sort of thoughtless, fruitless hours
The hangman has to spend alone. He'll maybe lop some flowers,
Or fix the pictures round the house, or, if a case is hotting
Up, he might in private fall to practising his knotting;
No matter what he does, no matter how he is inventive,
There's nothing in his occupation giving him incentive:
His bosses have ordered him 'on no account to phone us' –
And there isn't half a dog's chance of some overtime or bonus.

His occupation hasn't got a single whiff of glamour;
His customers are locked away inside a distant slammer;
Perhaps he dreams of Titipu, of posing on a rostrum,
But life, alas, is not like Art (a celebrated nostrum).
Anonymous, invisible, dependent on a jury
(A state that rouses any craftsman to a raging fury),
He has to keep his trap shut – God! it really must be awful,
Hanging round the home, and hoping they'll make your business lawful!

Bill Greenwell

Writing Free Verse for Auberon Waugh
Is hopeless. Verse that doesn't rhyme or beat
A rhythm like a bouncing basketball
Is given to the office goat to eat,
And sometimes heard as goat-burps down the hall.

K. Lloyd-Thompson

Absurd to Complain

Absurd to complain or try to maintain
That I am like wood
When this feels so good.

Absurd to say 'no, I really must go'
When your touch on my thigh is making me sigh.
Absurd to say 'no, I really must go'
When your lips on my skin make me want to begin.
Absurd to say 'no, I really must go'
When your hand on my breast makes me long for the rest.
Absurd to say 'no, I really must go'
When it's far, far too late and I simply can't wait.

Absurd to maintain or try to maintain
That you'll never undo me.
For God's sake, please screw me!

Hilary Mellon

Rape – Architects and Developers

Of Town Planners

They seem to roam the country like a band
Of plunderers, developing their themes
In brick and breeze block; any open land
Becomes the subject of their sordid dreams.
Perhaps they wonder, briefly, why the sane
Read ugliness between their tarmac lines,
Why even princes, blessed with half a brain,
Despise the crudity of their designs.
They banish drivers from the hearts of towns
To fill the street with sick geraniums;
Where do they live themselves? What circus clowns
Reside within their concrete craniums?
Only a crane with a massive iron ball
Could dent such skulls, and penetrate the wall.

Frank McDonald

Rape

'Well, accidents will happen'; or 'My men
Misunderstood instructions once again'.
It doesn't take a hurricane to raze
Two hundred years of growth in hours or days –
Bulldozers have the edge on acts of God
And *faits accomplis* pass through on the nod
With promises next time to toe the line
And covert presents, or at worst a fine.
Now picture windows will survey the scene
Not of a brook and trees but where they've been;

A further avenue of country seats
In three designs: the 'Wordsworth' or the 'Keats'
Or 'Byron' for the three-car family
Will fill the space reserved for greenery,
Since preservation orders are just words
And ponds and brush and copses 'for the birds',
There where the by-pass runs the land still bleeds
But speedy movement's what this village needs;
Since droving times the narrow winding street
Quietly helped the local heart to beat
Embodied by the church, the inn, the school,
Until transplanted under this new rule.

I have a feeling, though, the last word in
Will be from nature, for this thrifty skin
Of tarmac on the access roads now heaves
And through it poke fresh dandelion leaves.

Alanna Blake

Development

The earth is flattened for a built-up zone,
The very birds must take their pleasure higher;
The undergrowth by man is overgrown,
Fresh opening flowers laid waste with pick and fire.
Still buried deep, their seeds will lie and wait
Till he, that Faust whose greed brings tribulation,
Tires of the view his fitful ways create
And turns to yet more dangerous calculation.

One day these plants will grow in cleaner air,
And animals these builders never saw
Will roll and play about the clearing there,
Stirring the buried concrete with a paw.
Man will be gone; but so, I fear, will I;
I am the problem; I myself must die.

Paul Griffin

Leisure

Home Thoughts from Saudi Arabia

O listen, my darling, the lilac is stirring
The west wind blows soft on your sycamore tree
Soon under the cedar the tea-cups will glisten,
With brown bread and butter and strawberries for tea.

For surely our severance can't last for ever and
Long silver Sundays must one day return
To where on the margin, unnoticed, obscurely
The mark of the foam shows a tide on the turn.

My days as a rover will soon be over,
My contract be ended, the treasure be banked,
No phone calls no meetings but leisure for ever
To share with my sweeting, and Heaven be thanked.

Alec Peterson

Somewhere to Stay

I said to the man at the store,
I've travelled a lot in my time,
Through France to the Mediterranean,
From Spain to the banks of the Rhine.
    He said, well I've never gone far,
    Not more than from here to the bay,
    But I'm just about sure that I know
    Every inch of the ground on the way.

I told him I've seen all the shows,
Frequented the trendiest bars,
I've dined the most gorgeous of girls
And sat at the feet of the stars.
    He said, well as far as that goes
    We don't have no dancing girls here,
    But I mind a time in the meadow
    And the Plough serves a mighty good beer.

I mentioned how well I was blessed
With friends all over the place,
Friends in New York and Havana
Of every colour and race.
   He said, I've some good friends myself,
   Though none so far and so free,
   We don't in fact meet that often
   But they're all between here and the sea.

I said to the man at the store,
To be truthful I'm down in the mouth,
I miss all the glamorous evenings
And holidays spent in the South.
At night when it's dark I can slumber
And dream of the good days gone by,
Then I wake with a start in the morning
And the visions just dwindle and die.
   He said, the trouble with you
   Is that all you can see are your woes,
   And that's no great effort of vision
   Since they're stuck down the end of your nose.
   There are meadows and fields all around you,
   There's the forest way up on the hill,
   There's the pub for talking and drinking,
   There's the farm and the stream and the mill.

I said to the man at the store,
I'm afraid I'm a bit of a bore.
   Nonsense, he said, you're one of us now,
   Let's lock up the shop and slip round to the Plough.

John Bostock-Smith

A E I

The old piano's yellowed grin
Pounds out a quickstep; couples pass,
Exchanging glassy smiles, and spin
Away. The ballroom dancing class

Is ever-popular. Next door
A bluish haze hangs in the air
In strata; some pipe-smoking bore
Teaches philosophy in there.

In yoga, leotarded, they
Are straining to transcend the self;
Above them, lumps of unfired clay
Are lined up on the pottery shelf.

'Deux baguettes, s'il vous plait, madame',
They chorus from Beginners' French,
While right next door an oil-smeared arm
Shows how to use a monkey wrench.

In Cordon Bleu, the *petits fours*
Are overdone; an acrid pall
Drifts gently down the corridor
Towards the main Assembly Hall

Where 'Staging Shakespeare's Problem Plays'
Are stumbling through *Measure for Measure* . . .
So many multifarious ways
Of using up this thing called leisure . . .

Peter Norman

There's nothing I like better than a leisurely pursuit
Of men and women who have gained some singular repute
And wander incognito in a public place – a park,
Say, or a zoo where chimps and monkeys shin up concrete bark.
They've taken time off from their roles beneath some spotlit heat
To stroll along a by-way, wander down a simple street;
They're managers and statesmen who are prone to shouting odds,
Or actors who must strain their lungs when frowned on from the
     gods,
The powerful, in other words, who wish to take a rest
From fame and the necessity of looking at their best,
From lecturing, indeed, the likes of folk like me and you.
And these, I say, are just the ones I leisurely pursue.

I track them to their benches, where they rest their weary feet,
And treat themselves to privacy (they think!). Where they retreat,
It's often rather shady, fairly cool and not too loud:
They tend to haunt the fringes of a modest little crowd,
With hats that hide their features and a pair of polaroids
(And I'm the sort of fellow every one of them avoids).
They mooch, they smile, they pat their hands if offering applause –
If, say, a dolphin catches fish inside its open jaws –
And generally, these household names make very little fuss,
When normally they're as subtle as a blasted blunderbuss.
I once saw Terry Wogan walking round a village fête.
He tiptoed, mumbled, and his backbone wasn't very straight.

Now why, you ask, should I pursue these notables like this?
Do you suspect that I intend to catch them, take the piss,
Beg a fiver for my silence, and accept it with a laugh,
Or get stroppy and demand of them an outsize autograph?
How churlish of you! No, it's just that, when I'm on their trail
And they're concealing everything they elsewhere have on sale,
I find that they're adept at seeking out a secret spot
Where happy meditation is practicable. I'm not
A vicious little toady, or a spoilsport, or a fan
Who likes reflected glory for some basking where he can.
I'm merely one of those who think, and this with due respect,
That leisure is a skill possessed by most of the elect.

But if you're a mean, vindictive type who loathes celebrity,
I'll tell you this. You can't do worse than start to follow me.

Bill Greenwell

Anti-Racism

At infant school, some fifty years ago,
I wrote my News, about the local fair;
Of freaks and dodgems, and a boxing show,
Adding the words *there was a blackie there*.
My teacher pursed her lips, then kindly said,
'You mustn't call them that; they like to be
Called *coloured*.' This I filed inside my head
With other truths I'd garnered at her knee.
Now, I believe that *black* is deemed all right
Despite the fact it may be quite untrue,
But as for *coloured*, it could start a fight:
Miss Eatson's truths have faded with my dew.
    Too old to learn another lexicon,
    I shall just call them *people* from now on.

Noel Petty

This Spectr'd Isle

Civis sic Britannicus sum.
Come on here, there's stacks of room!
Repopulate our northern towns
Replace their workshy yobs and clowns.

Proud Britannia! Strong and free.
Let all nations welcome be
To England's shores, so mighty still,
To do those jobs we cannot fill.

Conduct a bus, run a shop,
Grease a nipple, be a cop.
We'll let you in the Guards one day,
The ranks, of course: that is our way.

Our friendly ways have drawn thanks
From Huguenots and even Yanks
Diggers, Taffs and guid Scots Laddies,
Kiwis, Canucks, papist Paddies.

Airman Poles who staunched the Blitz
Were welcomed back to man the pits,
And, at least for a little while,
Those volcanoed out of Tristan's isle.

They're kith and kin and fit in well.
House prices firm where'er they dwell.
You wouldn't fret if it should be
Your daughter brings one home to tea.

New Commonwealth's another matter.
Strange oriental cultures shatter
The way we've always lived and been,
Playing fair, God Save the Queen!

Asian chaps buy up houses
Our laws can't cope with all their spouses
And Afro-Caribbean squalls
Of reggae belt right through our walls.

Kingston, Georgetown, Port o' Spain,
Men from Leeward's island chain
Were welcome when we needed labour,
Not to stay to be our neighbour.

To live in peace is now our prayer,
To save the nation from despair.
A melting pot, soundly based on
Multi-cultural education.

Should lofty hopes go down the chute
Send home each Anglo, Saxon, Jute.

Derek Campbell

32

Blind Spot

I'm fond of a Darkie; I'm partial to Micks;
I'm also enamoured of Dagos and Spics.
There's only one race I would prejudge as pricks . . .
That's Americans.

Most Spades are outgoing and funny and nice.
Your Paki's hard-working, not given to vice.
And to dine *chez* the Frogs is to taste Paradise.
But . . . Americans!

They're pushy and schmaltzy and lacking in taste.
From New York to LA it's a cultural waste.
How can anyone 'Have a Nice Day' when he's faced
With Americans?

Macdonalds and Disney, Tom Sawyer and Huck,
Bill Cosby, John Wayne, Tweetie Pie, Donald Duck,
Those Barbie-Doll, Bambi-like Bimbos . . . oh yuck!

And the gat's always loaded, the Noon's always High:
The Bronx Robocops poke a gun in your eye:
Sylvester Stallone is a helluva guy
To Americans.

There's only a handful that I would excuse
(Like Mel Brooks and Perelman) had I to choose,
And one or two others – but those are all *Jews*,
Not Americans.

Colin Pearson

Growing Old

Sonnet (after Ronsard)

God only knows how little will remain
When we have time for candlelight and fires.
Memory in corners sketches the terrain
Of half-believed events, forlorn desires,
But tumbling words cannot recall the time,
Nor bring our history back within our sight.
'When you are old and grey', you will not climb
From some warm hearth to fetch, by candles' light,
Some book of verse which I will not have made;
Nor fawning servants start awake to praise
The never-written lines of one afraid
To bring despair upon your lonely days.
Remember, then, this 'poet' out of place,
And he, the unseen firelight on your face.

William Howard

Nunc Dimittis

Lord, now let your servant go in peace,
According to your word;
My eyes are tired, I long for my release
From a world become absurd
And bored with striving, in its last sad winding
Down to death's decay;
My youth spent in the joyous quest of finding
Truth is mocked. Dismay
Now haunts me, and I cannot bear contemplation
Of a world enchanted by its own annihilation.

Virginia Rounding

A Couple

A little breath; but then another slower:
Lion-hued grass adorns the lawn and mower.

The hours were handsome in their way, though they
Grew tired of how to be, and what to say.

A couple grows to one, though friends are lost
To life's too close attention, and the cost

Of just one metal-flash of scything stroke,
The reel, the peril of a single spoke,

Unhefts a grunting weight upon each mind.
Each cooked a pencil but was underlined

And summed: like wind they combed white chaff. Discreet
Appraisal had time walk on woman's feet

Back of the furrowed lines, the forehead wars:
Dabbling in her stock market, sharing scores

For ukelele ballads, moving books
Collected a near-century to low nooks

Reachable from his easy chair's hard rest.
Each morning it takes longer to get dressed.

Once, arm in arm, they halloed wheel-out babies
And crossed the lawn – not yet the walk. No maybes

Troubled the maple. Everything they saw
Moves like an unwound clock, the ancient maw;

Moot the last things against blade-silhouettes
Deafen within the wonder and old debts.

Where goes the sound of lucky, peaceful hours?
The wrinkling mane is combed out of the flowers,

The walk swept. Present and past tenses curl
A grandchild's age into their age; a swirl
Of magic-sequinned air precipitates:
A slower breath tucked in awaits, awaits.

Joel Graham

Love on a Pension

Come stay with me. The night is drawing near.
It's only four o'clock and light,
Like life, has disappeared.

Be by my side. I'm cold and cloistered here.
A single pension's not enough
When winter turns severe.

Don't freeze me out. I'm longing to be charmed.
The passions that we might ignite
Could keep us both well-warmed.

Be kind to me. Pretend I'm your desire.
I'm wrinkled, but I'll straighten out
When both of us retire.

Bring all your shillings. Feed them to the fire.
Turn up the gas and let it blaze
Before we both expire.

K. Lloyd-Thompson

Sonnet

And does it end like this, quite, quite alone,
The island Donne denied most surely there,
And fractured hope that time cannot postpone,
All bridges broken and the landscape bare?
And does it end like this, with memory's store
A perjured rose and echoes of a sigh,
And all the promised paths that were no more
Than terraces to castles-in-the-sky?
By loss or by desertion we are left
Without the unity of former ways,
The past annulled, the future quite bereft,
Alone within the prison of our days.
Apart, we watch life's pageantry pass by,
The shadow-people queuing up to die.

Helen Forsyth

Betrayal

Betrayal

Walk on the waves? Change water into wine?
We sank, of course, or tasted water still.
Buying the premise that a Great Design
Requires a Designer, we would kill
For the trinkets they sold us.
Miracles were just a page away
From comic strips and childish tragedies.
Believing the panacea was to pray,
We soon discovered that our Arcadies
Were not what they told us.

Yet who deceived us? Was it prudish Paul
Or Lot, or David with Goliath's head?
What of that awesome writing on the wall?
Mere superstition? Why were we misled
By such a plot?
We scanned the heavens looking for a sign,
Grew cynical, and took to Kant and Hume.
Our earthly wisdom cancelled our divine,
Preferring the sage acceptance that the tomb
Keeps what it's got.

When ghosts of doubt arose we shook our heads,
We were too worldly wise to swallow twice;
We spend our Sunday mornings in our beds
Chuckling at fools who needed priests' advice.
We knew the traps!
And yet we still go back with greying thought
To the primal tunes our infancy heard played,
Wondering why a lesson, poorly taught,
Still hints of hidden truths we have betrayed
In a poem . . . perhaps.

Frank McDonald

37

'The heart has more rooms than a whorehouse.'

Haggard, raddled, madam memory winks,
Ushers me, hesitant, into her red plush hall.
The girls glance up, turn, hide their false smiles' fall:
Madam nods to Margit to fetch drinks.
Some find reasons, others just say 'no':
Sheila puts her glasses on to read;
Monika bares a pale white breast, to feed
Her son, my rival, as the others go.
Last, hot fury: scorning regret and doubt,
Judy folds her cold blue gown to rise,
Point, pass judgement from electric eyes:
She spits 'You bastard!', sweeps, majestic, out.
We drain our glasses. Madam cocks her head,
Leads me, unprotesting, to her bed.

Simon Darragh

Betrayed

I thought I'd write a bitter-sweet tirade
To pierce the leather binding of your heart
On how you shuffled off, left me betrayed.

Perhaps you thought my love would start to fade,
That time and distance both would play their part,
Until I felt resigned, and not betrayed.

But I'm not made of shabby old brocade
That moths and dust will gently tear apart:
I was the flesh and blood on whom you preyed.

I was the instrument whose tunes you played –
And played, I well remember, with some art,
To make duets that earned your accolade.

I thought at last I'd really made the grade,
Believed that this was *really* Cupid's dart;
I never knew you'd be a renegade.

No plaques will mark the hotel where we stayed,
And where we walked the shadow-prints depart
Like ghosts on winter's empty esplanade.

Now I am sadder, wiser, still afraid,
Breaking this circle for another start;
To let you know I know I'd been betrayed
I thought I'd write. A bitter-sweet tirade.

D. A. Prince

From whispers in high places
To gossip in the street,
From thirty coins of silver
To blackmail's balance sheet,
From national disloyalty
To personal betrayal
England and the English
Are constantly for sale.

If not for love or money,
Then jealousy or fear
Will keep the home tongues wagging
To any open ear.
As secrets are transmitted
And skeletons revealed
One yearns to know of someone
Whose lips are truly sealed.

As characters are blackened
Or murdered by degrees
By those who own to friendship,
Why talk of enemies?

Katie Mallett

Sonnet

O traitorous, self-regarding Modern Poet!
Betrayer of Calliope, thy Muse!
If you respect her Rhyme you rarely show it:
Her Scansion you most wilfully abuse.
Such Form your genius palpably despises,
Scorning the paths of bards who went before.
And do you feel you'll carry off more prizes
As long as you're sufficiently obscure?
Why are your messages to esoteric
They can't in rhyme and rhythm be expressed?
Is yours some vision that escaped, say, Herrick?
Or Keats and Donne and Marvell and the rest?
If Shakespeare stooped to court and wins his muse,
Why can't you bend a little, Mr Hughes?

Colin Pearson

She saw the tortured body of her son
Some hours before his death, his nineteenth year
Distorted by man's cruelty and fear.
Friends said, 'You saw. You were the lucky one.'

Children were turned to silence, words to blows,
All questions were forbidden by the state
And sleepless longing settled down to wait
For news that maybe someone, somewhere knows.

Meanwhile, in Britain, poets, line by line,
Seep out permitted words for love or gain,
Offered, as a reward for all their pain –
So generous – a case of Chile's wine.

Kathleen Bell

First and Last Loves

First and Last Love

Snow at the window-pane, ghosts in the chimney,
Secrecy, silence, adults asleep.
Moon through the darkness, stars like an army,
Breakers complaining way out in the deep.
Was there a stirring of ego-awareness,
A point where the shadows conceded to light?
Here was the cradle of love in its rareness,
Teaching the child to get used to the night.

Rich candelabra, a mystical setting,
Litanies, litanies . . . *ora pro quo?*
Rows of grey reverence, whispering, fretting,
Here were the stirrings of love long ago.
Out in the darkness, a glance at the chapel,
Footsteps resentful of why they should leave,
Feelings of something, as tall as the steeple,
Love was the taste of an old Christmas Eve.

Here comes the Magus, miles from Bethlehem,
Attracted to something he heard in the air,
Was it a carol, or was it a requiem,
After a lifetime he really won't care.
Who knows the difference, loving or leaving,
What was the something his lips tried to say?
Snow at the window-pane, ghosts in the chimney,
Love's still a mystery – keep it that way!

Frank McDonald

First and Last Loves

These I first loved: syrup of figs;
Aniseed balls, pink sugar pigs;
Crunchy cream meringues; eclairs;
My shabby family of teddy bears;
A rubbery giraffe, large, pale and bendy;
A neighbour's straight-haired daughter, Wendy;
The secret bedtime reading of some story;
The garishness of Knickerbocker Glory;
My mother's sweet carnation scent;
My spaniel, Mick; sleeping in a tent;
And crawling to see the midnight stars;
Long Sunday picnic trips in cars,
First, primroses, then blackberries and nuts;
Tiger Tim's Weekly; *Comic Cuts*;
Long walks on the Downs; Lott's bricks;
My first full box of conjuring tricks
(I saw myself, starring on the Halls,
Producing silk flags and glittering coloured balls).

These then were my loves, these the first.
My last loves? These I've not rehearsed.
What might they be? This all depends
Upon the way my journey ends.
My wife, of course; I trust that she'll be there,
And with her, all the other loves we share.
What else? My pipe, my talking-book machine;
The feel of beauty that's no longer seen,
The taste of luxury I can't afford?
The sister of some geriatric ward?
I'd like some music when I really go:
A Beethoven quartet and *Figaro*.
There will be friends, all the best I know –
These let me love, then let me swiftly go.

E. O. Parrott

First Love/Last Love

Tree branches whip like skipping ropes,
Whine through the windy evening air.
Rain splashes as my boyfriend gropes
Inside my dress, but I don't care,
My love has warmed this cold dark park,
Inflamed me with its first bright spark.

Whispered words and giggles merge
With secret kisses on the grass,
Giving in to nature's urge –
But just so far – a tangled farce
Of fear, frustration and desire,
Of inbred guilt and first love's fire.

Now like a well worn shabby pair
Of slippers by the hearth we sit,
Each settled in a favourite chair
To read, or watch TV, or knit.
Words are few, and kisses less,
But neither doubts our happiness.

Familiar now, each fond caress
As gentle as a summer breeze,
An unexpressed likemindedness
Transcends all language boundaries
As in our last love's harmony
We wait for heaven's ecstasy.

Katie Mallett

Love on the Move

To merit deep love, one must be
Combustible internally.

A man matures and shares his heart
When pistons throb and motors start.

He's fickle, his affection steals
To anything upon four wheels.

The clapped-out Mini is the best
Proving at least he's passed the test.

And next, to gain experience, he
Goes for a veteran MG.

Now he divorces, none too soon,
The little family saloon.

In Italy and then Japan
His favour's cosmopolitan.

When middle age begins to drag
He briefly has a speeding Jag;

Then more sedate, to settle down,
Takes a Mercedes up to town,

Till limited by wealth and age
He passes to the Escort stage.

His last love overtakes the first –
In a black Roller he is hearsed.

Alanna Blake

First and Last Loves

I was seven, he was twenty three:
Accomplices were we.
He'd stay out all night;
I'd throw down the key.
(My parents dead, his had adopted me,
Aspiring saints to be.)
But then they found him out
And sent him off to sea.

(Many men I later had
And many men had me;
Many men I've driven mad,
And many men set free:
And each liaison left me sad
Because of him — at sea.)

I'm sixty-seven now, he eighty-three:
Spent lovers both are we,
Remembering, each night
How, then, we'd held the key
To unlock joy and let our passion free
To meet in ecstasy.
Now, we're deaf. We shout
In perfect harmony.

Richenda Miers

Outrage and Racehorses

It is a special constable,
And he stoppeth one in three.
'By what authority and right,
And wherefore stopp'st thou me?'

'Well, as to why I stopped you,
And since you ask what's what,
The orders from our Chief are
To breathalyse you lot.'

'Breathtaking bloody cheek, I say,
Your Chief can go to hell;
And, breathing fire and brimstone,
He'll find me there as well.'

Angus Hill

Outrage

'It's long I've been waiting, oh Algy my dear,
And the dinner's been spoiling for ages I fear.
What kept you so long?' 'An impertinent cuss
Who, after the races, breathalysed us.'
'You're not caught again?' 'No, never you fear –
So long in the queue gave my breath time to clear.
But how dare he subject us to such third degree?
When I've finished this drink I'll ring up my MP.'

'You're late from the races, oh Billy my son,
Your neck is all twisted, you're pale as a bone.'
'Oh mother, my mother, I've found a cold bed,
With dirt in my mouth and a stone at my head.
Throw out my slippers, throw away my high tea,
The driver who hit me had his last drink on me.'

B. M. Kaye

Stewards' Enquiry

How rich it is to contemplate
The strange vicissitudes of Fate,
Which oft subvert mere human plan
(Especially for the betting man).

Take Royal Ascot, second day.
The two o'clock is under way.
The favourite's jockey (claiming 7)
Is somewhere on the M11.

A substitute is in the plate,
But carries two pounds overweight.
That's why (the pundits must suppose)
The favourite's beaten by a nose.

And consequently, for my sins,
My 12 to 1 outsider wins.
And had it not, M'Lud, been so
I'd not have ordered Veuve Clicquot.

The next race goes the way I'd reckoned
(Or we should not have had the second).
The fourth result was too absurd
(Which seemed to justify the third).

The sun was hot. The sky was blue.
The last romped home at 5 to 2.
Of course we had to toast The Queen:
And that is why the bag turned green.

This life of roundabouts and swings!
The sheer vicissitude of things!
The mystic ways of Fate, or God,
I tried to share with PC Plod.

Ah, fickle Chance! I quickly saw
The said custodian of the law
(However swift my darlings ran)
Was not, M'Lud, a betting man.

Colin Pearson

47

God and Joy

I wonder, did George Herbert sweep a room,
Or hang out washing on a winter's day?
The first task clouds the mind with certain gloom,
The second makes it difficult to pray.

A poet who has never tasted graft
Can prate of work in syllables sublime.
He plies a cerebral and gentle craft,
And never marks his hands with oil or grime.

How easily he defies the dull,
When sheltered from the boredom of routine,
He meditates, for here is time to mull
His idle thoughts, or act the libertine.

When days stretch out in slow monotony,
With little to alleviate the view,
How does one picture God in botany,
Where flowers are far between and very few?

One needs the patience of a Trappist monk,
The genius of a Michelangelo,
To see all heaven in a heap of junk,
Or reap from toil a holy afterglow.

Patricia V. Dawson

Gaudebimus, igitur!

Praise be to God for inconspicuous things:
For little men who tend their plots with pride,
For laughing-eyed pursuits and wedding rings,
And unexplored domains where pleasures hide,
Night footsteps on the streets where childhood sings
Of heavens our hasty thoughts once cast aside;
Praise be to God for that persistent light
That tempted us to be his acolyte.

Those melodies in rhododendron shade
That lull us to the comfort of belief
Send forth our thoughts to land where Adam played,
Closing our hearts to envy or to grief;
And pondering how our searching has been paid
With evening hope (however all too brief),
We find our answers in a sunset sky,
The long-sought whispers of a youthful 'why'.

Another sunlight, warmer than the rest,
Dispels the fears of unexplained despair,
The foolish urge to be among the best
Is out of place upon a garden-chair;
We laugh at dreams of climbing Everest,
(We who are breathless as we mount the stair)
And after years of seeking a different rhyme
We know the truth was with us all the time.

Praise be to God (wherever he resides)
For leaving us to colour in his sketch,
For having us desert our inner pride
To glimpse the love that we could never reach;
The very hurt that once we sought to hide
Is now the corner-stone of what we preach:
Praise be to God for inconspicuous things,
And listening, when a third-rate singer sings!

Frank McDonald

Forbidden Love

Let us have no more nonsense of hypocrisy and cant,
There's a natural law of things, no matter how the parsons rant;
There's a method in the madness of the comic, cosmic plan,
And if you were not a woman I could never be a man.

There's a type of whining sickness that's a parody of truth,
That mocks maturity, and marks the crippling of youth;
That robs an eye of lustre, and that stains an honest lust
With the ashen hue of ashes, and the dustiness of dust.

Thank God for honest passion, for the blood that wells to blind,
With a bursting of the body and a palsy of the mind;
Thank God for Nature's reason, which in spite of cant believes
In a multitude of Adams and a myriad of Eves.

My God is Pan, the Earth-God; he is horned and furrow-faced;
His virtue is fulfilment, and his wickedness is waste;
All the Mad-May-morning madness he will see and not be shocked,
But there's mockery in moonlight, and my God will not be mocked.

His shrine where I should worship is wherever I may be,
But I made a graven image of your youth and chastity;
And the mark of his displeasure is the drowning flood he pours
On the million lives within me that are calling out to yours.

For my Earth-God is a wrathful God of jealousy and greed
Who will visit his displeasure on the sinner and his seed;
And his anger is upon me, that I would not seek the prize
That was promised in the shining understanding of your eyes.

What fools our Gods must think us, that our three-score years and ten
Are thrown up on the altar of the muddled minds of men;
Our span is but a flutter of their swift, capricious wings,
Yet our greatest rule of virtue is the permanence of things.

Thank God for every moment that allows another breath,
For beyond our share of moments is the permanence of death;
O God of mine, forgive me for the time I held her fast,
And I let her go unloved, because I knew it could not last.

Did you know then how I loved you in the moment that was mine?
Did you feel my fingers fevering to twine and intertwine?
Could you not have made that single hour a sacrifice to Pan,
For the glory of your womanhood, because I was a man?

We can talk of creed and principle, and ponder in our pride
On our subtle suffocation of a mood that lived and died;
But we never could excuse, although we took the whole of time,
The miracle we buried in a civilising slime.

Allan Warbis

Feeling Fruity

Buggery's accepted now.
Let out of the closet
Gays can make a 'marriage' now
And place a house deposit.
But woe betide the chap who yearns
To find some sexual joy
(Though mutual lust or passion burns),
With some young willing boy.

Kissing cousins are OK,
Though still one must resist a
Stray or constant urge to lay
One's brother or one's sister.
Girls of fourteen go along
To the FPA for pills,
But the guys who partner them do wrong,
And may face prison's ills.

51

Copulating with a sheep
Is frowned upon, but still
One can abuse one's wife to reap
Some cheap orgasmic thrill.
Who does what and who has whom
Is a trivial press pursuit,
But even tabloids don't give room
To those who lust for fruit.

For grapes are quite insentient,
And grapefruit passion free,
And even sucking with intent
Invites no penalty.
Oranges will never kiss
And tell (though juicy stuff),
Bananas never prejudice
One's health by being rough.

In no place does the Good Book state
That fruit love is disowned,
Not even those who fornicate
With dates will end up stoned.
Yet at the centre lies a seed
Of guilt, as conscience ridden
One tries to fill the human need
Of taking what's forbidden.

Katie Mallett

Forbidden Love

The times are out of joint; no more, my love,
In innocence we loiter in full view.
Now doors are closed against us. From Above
The edict comes 'We'll tread upon the likes of you'.

No longer publicly I press your white-sheathed form
Against my lips, inhale your perfume sweet.
My vegetable love becomes the butt of scorn;
Disgrace and shame now stalk us in the street.

Friends turn aside and look the other way,
Shaking their heads in sorrow; drop their eyes
And shed a tear if we're too close, and say
'It won't be long before that Unregenerate dies'.

Well maybe so and maybe not. Dear friend
Who cheers my downcast hours, brings so much joy,
I shall be faithful to the very end.
My final breath you'll share; I'm Fortune's toy.

For one more burning kiss I ever lust,
Another lung-filled drag on pleasure called obscene.
What boots it if our mingled ashes turn to dust?
For joyless so will theirs, in time, my Nicotine.

Caroline Pugh

Why did we have to meet for the first time
Exactly half-an-hour after your wedding?
The jolly bells had barely ceased to chime
When, entering that flash hotel in Reading
That Mother chose for Angela's Reception
We saw each other. Saw and loved – too late,
With instant, fearless, mutual perception.
Why did you choose her? Why didn't you wait?

But if you hadn't gone for Angela
I shouldn't have come home from Tenerife,
I planned to travel on to Africa
Not to come back to play the role of thief.
Somehow I might have stood there and contrived
A social pantomime – caught the bouquet
Perhaps – but how long could I have survived?
And you . . . You nearly gave yourself away.

I'm sure you wanted me to understand
And that was easy. I had seen your soul
Drain from your eyes to lie within your hand
As we were introduced, and so made whole.
In that first handshake we exchanged our vows
Though no one knows the agony we feel
Between the little spaces God allows
For us to meet in, to unite and heal.

Ginger Jelinek

Not now to mention, that once golden one,
Who walked with me in moonlight, years gone by;
Though contact's lost, and all repining's done,
Yet heart, demanding, still reproaches, Why?

This other she, this wife of loyal years,
Sits out fulfilment, child on child, content,
For her no sorrows, no remembered tears,
No agonising over passion spent.

Age tugs at tissues, tires the mind,
We sit in wedlock, cosy and replete,
And yet that other love intrudes, and still I find
Echoes of heels come tapping down the street.

Which is illusion. Love does not survive
In separation. Old men count their pence;
It now takes care for me to keep alive,
And everything squares off to commonsense.

Yet, once, I came to first requited kiss,
Leapt, tiptoed, sang, made arabesque,
Thought joy eternal – now it comes to this –
Shrunk, shrivelled, silent, elderly, grotesque.

So I hold silence. Nothing to confess.
She knits, I read, no mutual secret harms:
And yes, we come to harbour, happiness,
But oh, that other softness in my arms!

Harold V. S. Page

In Praise of France

Liberté

Is it the wine, the cigarettes
That fill the air with scented smoke
Ungoverned yet by unveiled threats
Or warnings of disease, the folk,
Old ladies dressed in black, in fields
Bending over harvests, men
With leather faces talking yields
From fields, or boule, or playing again
The latest football match, the blue
Of the Côte d'Azure, unsmeared by clouds,
Or maybe the untainted view
From mountains unassailed by crowds?
Or maybe the Camargue, the waste
Run through by horses, and the wild
Wild open spaces of sky enlaced
With seabirds? Like a hungry child
I long for France, to taste and feel
Its freedoms, shielded by the zeal
Of governors with hands of steel.

Katie Mallett

Disappointment

The Poem Always Disappoints

The poem's image: Escher-sharp, defined,
Seen in an instant's waking, sunlit clear,
Original, ready for grasping, mere
Words away: a butterfly, outlined

Against a window. Practised stealth, an art
Learned out of books, the writer's fine-meshed net
Teased round frail quivering wings, so slowly, yet
Somehow a hand slipped, jogged the stunning dart.

It looks a bit bedraggled on the page.
Pinned down, spread flat, the colour's somewhat smudged,
The lines no longer sharp, as though they grudged
Captivity. Museum-labelled – age,

Date, provenance. Quite tidy, but the stink
Of ether clings. A botch job, once again.
The image, second-rate, slips off the pen.
A broken chrysalis. Not worth the ink.

D. A. Prince

Ode to a Trim-phone

Why won't you ring? –
You stubborn, hard, and silent
Dark blue thing –
Why won't you ring?

You sit there on the floor, serene,
Self-satisfied and very mean,
Aware that just one tiny bleep
From you would make my spirits leap.

You have me at your mercy, yes
You do, and to a cruel excess
You use your selfish skill –
So quiet, trim, and coldly still.
To think that I, who once so proud
Would spurn the influence of a crowd,
Am now obsessed by one so small,
Am at this object's beck and call.
You outstare me – I cannot win,
Can never fight that knowing grin;
And so I turn, pretend to read
And try to lose the urgent need
To hear you ring –
You stubborn, hard, and silent
Dark blue thing.

I read, and finally begin
To see the words again, and win
Back self-control. And then you ring.
I fling
My book aside and hear, perplexed,
'Hello? Is Keith there? Is that Keith?'
Past caring now, I sink my teeth
Into your hateful flex.

Virginia Rounding

Disappointment

The room is in rank, indisputable gloom
As the news is announced to the leader. A hush
Like the last, rasping gasp of a mantis's groom
Fills his thoughts. And at once, an inordinate rush

Of the bloodied and bandaged come bang in his head;
There explode in his memory carnival dreams.
Where a pavement was decked, falls the rain. Where the dead
Were extolled, lies a body which swelters and steams.

In the rage of outrageous assaults on the sky,
On the ramparts he'd hung with impossible flags,
His future unfurled, and flew proudly on high.
There were flames in his hair. Now doused, as he sags

In a pitch where a posse of corporal louts
Arrive panting for power. Each smothers his face
With Gethsemane kisses, condolences, doubts
That the rumours are true ('which would be a disgrace').

His fatigues start to reek. There is rust on his blade,
And his stallion of marble is suddenly air.
There is dirt on his collar, and dust on his braid.
His heroics are tame, and his rhetoric bare

Of those elegant touches which . . . smart as a lash,
A new messenger strides to the centre of stage.
He is gaunt, but the crowd see him cutting a dash.
His name (on his lips) may embellish the page

Of a history written to garnish this trite,
Undistinguished scintilla of time. With his lids
Hid in shadow, he heads for the urinous light.
It is time for the leader to gamble. He bids

The intruder to speak in a powerful voice.
Let the words he'll sound out be as loud, and as clear
As the waves on a reef. The moment is choice:
The newcomer brags that there's nothing to fear.

A setback, an injury – minor. A nick
On the boss of the shield, on the butt of a gun,
On the flesh of a shoulder. The missive is quick:
The battle thought lost may now daily be won.

With a shrug of indifference, the child turns his back
On the playground, a terrible roar as before
Now ringing his ears. Was the moment so black?
Meant his nemesis, end? Disappointing, no more.

Bill Greenwell

Disappointment

Though moon and stars may rhapsodise above her,
Her charm and beauty do my heart bemuse;
I find no words to tell her how I love her,
So we discuss the weather and the news.

Through darkling lanes we wander side by side,
While moonbeams silvertip each leaf and plant;
And I, with trembling thrill I scarce can hide,
Whisper sweet passages from Freud and Kant.

Betimes we crouched beneath a sheltering bush,
While lightning cleft the sky with wicked swords,
The heavens wept with pain; and in the hush
I read to her the latest score from Lords.

What joyous times we have when we are roaming;
We're strolling out this evening, by the by.
What's this? A hurried note! She isn't coming,
And won't meet me again! . . . I wonder why?

Allan Warbis

Anxiety

On Reading Virginia Woolf's Diary for Monday 23 June 1919

When Mrs Woolf confesses
Her deepest inner fear
Is not reviews, but dresses,
I raise an answering cheer.

I'd thought remote Virginia
Above such worldly fret;
Mind higher, body skinnier
That common reader, yet

With *Night and Day* fresh printed
The problem pressing on
Is not reviews, new-minted,
But clothes for Garsington.

And here she shows her stress: would
Her new blue dress excel?
Her prime concern: the dress should
Charm Ottoline Morrell.

This diary's private writing
Reveals the human face;
Not Bloomsbury inter-fighting
But this most common-place –

What woman finds so painful,
What shames her to despair,
While man can be disdainful
She worries what to wear.

Let feminists probe why it is,
I'm reassured: here's why.
We share the same anxieties,
Virginia Woolf and I.

D. A. Prince

Dies Irae

I search for signs beneath the lines
Of life's perplexing tale,
Treat old despairs with older prayers
And day by day I fail;
I try to look beyond the book,
Afraid that fate might close it,
But still I seem to find one theme,
And wonder how I chose it.

I sometimes know that subtle glow
Of truth beyond my vision,
But fear the shame that speaks its name
To boredom, or derision;
Though in the end I meekly bend
To make a coward's denial,
An inner sense builds my defence
For when I stand on trial.

Will I review the things I do
With Rhadamanthine eyes,
And judge as nought the dreams I thought
Were grandeur in disguise?
Was fate's caress a game of chess
With passed pawns, never queening?
Will all the hours that fear devours
Be poems that have no meaning?

I fear that day when fate will say:
'Cast every word aside,'
And what was done will make me burn
In sorrow, not in pride.
I fear the eyes that might despise
In the Ultimate Review
No favoured mind, but someone blind,
A poet, a parvenu.

Frank McDonald

Anxiety

My aunty dusts her slippery Melamine,
Fluffs the pampas on the mezzanine –
Armed with her *Woman's Own*, she sits and rages,
Not daring to break the quiet by turning pages.
Despite all this, the house is tuning in:
The microwave, the Magimix begin
To pulse their menace down the wires –
Prescience of radioactive fires.
The cordless phone relays a hollow squeak,
The central heating thermostat will speak
Of happy progress on domestic skies,
Of ozone-friendly lead-free pies.
The ultimate full-function bedside clock,
Provides a thrilling and ecstatic shock!
The sewing-machine, a Singer in its youth,
Is set to make amends for the awful truth –
My aunty's static polyester dress
Lures the very waves of her distress.
For she's rarely wholly in control
As the tin-foil loosens on its roll
And earthquakes in the underfloor cables
Ambush the legs of occasional tables.

Then in Neutral Earth the tiny voices
Metallic and in song:
'You've made a thousand careful choices,
And every one of them was wrong.'

Helen Flint

Anxiety

'Who is that man against the wall?
The tall man standing there,
Under the wall-light in the shade
With the dandelion hair.'

'He always comes at tea-time
And Olly I'm afraid
His teeth are white and smiling
Under the blue lamp-shade.

The long nights do not scare me
Nor the pain beneath the skin
The only thing that bothers me
Is the smiling teeth and him.

He will not go at midnight
He will not go till three
And then we go together
To the black and shining sea.'

Austin Johnson

Anxiety
(Small Great War memorial near Vimy Ridge)

Outside, a wandering tractor goes
Politely ploughing round the edge.
Inside is altogether calmer
Than the hot roadway; lilac grows
Within a very formal hedge
(Doubtless a nuisance for the farmer).

The letters cut in marble shew
The limits of existence – then.
This they could never quite foretell.
Around such amphitheatres grow
Fat roses, roots in shredded men;
Landscaped in a crater, echo-shell.

Years back, completely hidden now
Alike from airless, day-bright June,
Or distant diesel's muted clatter,
Or lawns set down amidst the plough,
Stood simple men (though all too soon
A shell – just one – resolved the matter).

Waiting for 'Zero', for 'the off',
Pressed to the trench's wall, they know
How slowly move the hands upon
Their CO's watch, while mortars cough
Their contribution to the slow
Agony of barrage. All now gone

Or buried, save an anxious sense
That we, politely on the edge
Of long-spent hours preceding battle,
Misunderstand such moments dense
With fearfulness. Once, near this hedge,
Stood dumbly frightened men, like cattle.

So came the shell, thus to convert
Them into 'sacrificial youth'.
These vanished in one lyddite breath,
Hiding their reasons in the dirt
But leaving one unlovely truth:
Silence is the sweetest gift of death.

Janet Raden

(Note: Lyddite is a high explosive, much used in the Great War.)

In Praise of Cats

Egyptian Cat

Observe the window edged and veiled with lace.
Your cat, who lies in curves to fit the bay
Watches the minutes spiral through the day,
The people moving through a thin, grey space,
And in the houses opposite, pale lights like yellow eyes.

I am her ancestor. My eyes are blind
And in this pose I was designed to stand
Thousands of years ago. A sculptor's hand
Pushed me towards the cat-shape in his mind.
Like waves outside my small glass tomb, the sands of desert rise.

Adèle Geras

Gran Rifiuto

A fish-wife gull gapes wide her beak to scream,
Lets fall a cod's head on the grass below.
Rizzini on his fence perceives its gleam,
Receives its perfume on the air-stream's flow.

With ginger fur of which he's justly vain,
Inflamed by rare desire, in crouched mistrust,
He circles, stalks and circles yet again.
He feigns bravura, mimics unknown lust.

Deprived in kittenhood of cat-hood's fire,
Not risking hunting, used to feline jeers,
When Crow swashbuckles near in black attire,
Rizzini glares, turns tail and disappears.

Unkind, this life, to over-cautious souls
Who long to reach, but won't defend their goals.

Margaret Harris

Feles Angelicus

He purrs black thoughts, his long satanic stare
Stirs magic from the dawn of ancient days;
Infernal flames of some occult affair
Flicker within the firelight of his gaze.
He shuts his eyes, returning to his lair
In dark internal jungles where he plays;
And I presume to call this creature mine,
Whose world is closed, whose steps I can't confine.

Sometimes I sense a murder in his eyes:
Some morning bugler silenced by his claws,
Or evening singer taken by surprise
That lived within the terror of his laws.
He sleeps beside me, wearing his disguise
Of angel innocence on silent paws,
And as I contemplate some slaughtered dove
He soothes such fears with artificial love.

Sennacherib had stroked these sleeping limbs,
And pharaohs praised their dark divinity,
The fall of Rome was captured in the rims
Of feline eyes, that knew eternity;
Have they grown cold on all the savage hymns
That man has used to mock his deity?
Such minds, perhaps, have power to understand
The cosmos buried in Blake's grain of sand.

They rush away, like yesterday's delight,
Beyond the call of man's priority,
And sport with death in rituals of night
As though they stalked with God's authority.
When they return, their silent stares recite
Their hidden crimes with cunning clarity,
Like poems that hide their author's true intent
Yet show enough to hint at what was meant.

Frank McDonald

Nine Lives

Swirling in the accustomed place,
The fish tail gleams with light;
The cat's tail swishes too; its face
Gazes intent upon the sight.

Upon Gray's poem I reflect:
Perhaps she'll make a dash, and drown;
Perhaps my study will be wrecked;
But they relax, and settle down.

Fish, cat, and I, we travel on,
Leading nine lives of no event,
Of irritations come and gone,
Of sudden crises quickly spent.

I love the cat, the cat loves fish,
The fish loves food, we all love posing.
Why should I wish my cat and fish
Should know that all our lives are closing?

For soon my fish, for lack of cover,
Will meet the death with which he's flirted,
And you, my puss, will with your lover
To common pasture be converted.

Till then, we love and feign our crises;
We purr, and sleep, and sniff the weather;
Sheathing our talons and our vices
We pad along our lives together.

We tell ourselves that we're in clover;
Then that cold river multiplex
Winds in our path, the dark mist over,
And breaks our journey, and our necks.

Paul Griffin

Tramp

Infernal cat! You shame me endlessly,
Among the queenly beasts that smoothly hunt
These well-bred terraces and flaunt their charms
Like bathing beauties on the waterfront.

What foolish cat but you, with drooling lips,
Would bring a fillet steak clamped in your jaws,
The butcher's bill still clinging to the flesh;
Then trip me up and madly seek applause.

And self-respecting cats should slink or glide,
Moving with power controlled by stealthy feet;
Not thump like elephants at eventide,
Dislodging slates and waking all the street.

Independent chauvinistic tom,
You are unique. Alas you'll always be.
For I, in whom you placed your wary trust,
Betrayed your manhood, irreversibly.

John Bostock-Smith

Salvation

Gifts

Tearless at the death of Santa Claus —
His makeweights in the stocking showed
Frugality, and labels from the local stores,
No sleighbells rattled, and it never snowed

And even a greedy child has pride —
I sang a secret joyous song instead
Having long suspected that my parents lied
And glad to know the jolly monster dead.

Too soon I celebrated freedom though.
For next they taught me of a God who pried
Too deep in my innermost thoughts, and who
I equally wished to throw aside,

Who demanded I be good, believe as well
In one who offered what I'd not be given
Though I was less afraid of Satan's hell
Than all the promises He gave of heaven.

And so it goes on all life long,
There's always some salvation crew
Who never think they might be wrong
Or doubt they know what's good for you,

Who haunt with promises the ample air,
Line second-best gifts along the shelf
Though salvation or damnation is one's own affair,
The best gifts are those one gives oneself.

R. J. Caldwell

Salvation

I wish I had a rapier wit,
A brilliant and incisive mind
To keep my end up, just a bit,
But somehow I get left behind.

I've shot my conversational bolt
With just one glass of gin and tonic:
My tiny mind, in mute revolt,
Has frozen in a haze moronic.

Some casual, multilingual phrase
Indicative of education
Would steer me through this dreadful maze
Of intellectual conversation.

Instead, I listen with respect
While more sophisticated wives
Discuss the work of Bertolt Brecht,
The compositions of Charles Ives.

I turn my apprehensive mind
And bright, bright smile upon my right.
This face, I see at once, is kind –
But *oh*! His forehead! What a *height*!

Those shrewd and penetrating eyes
I'm sure are measuring my IQ
He asks me, should Heath compromise?
And what the IMF should do . . .

Oh! *Saved*! An old friend, by the fire.
I settle down with huge relief
And for a nice relaxing hour
Discuss the shocking price of beef.

Pamela Holden

Salvation

I live in poverty
Saves me from spending.

I never borrow
Saves me from lending.

I lie awake
Saves me from sleeping.

I laugh a lot
Saves me from weeping.

I stare around
Save me from blinking.

I act on impulse
Saves me from talking.

I lounge about
Saves me from walking.

I haven't a watch
Saves me from timing.

I write free verse
Saves me from rhyming.

I take no lovers
Saves me from lying.

I'll commit suicide
Save me from dying.

R. J. Pickles

Judges and Judging

Croker

It was an afternoon of bitter sleet
Whipping his windows in the granite street
When Croker for some reasons of his own
Decided to destroy *Endymion*.
First he worked out a highly merry quip
About John Keats and 'Cockney' authorship;
Then he declared that, if it had a plot
(Which he much doubted), it was utter rot;
Next he averred the ghosts of *bouts-rimés*
Had driven his witless maunderings astray;
Then that he couldn't scan; then that his taste
For minting words was hideously misplaced:
In short John Keats had better sheathe his pen,
And take a pint of port, and think again.
An hour well spent; he gave his specs a rub,
Then off to join Will Gifford in the club.

But soon in shining Rome the inky shade
Of a tall cypress crept along the bed
That glimmered like a white barge in the room,
Bearing the lord of language to his doom;
And there above him, all those words that live,
The *Odes*, the *Pot of Basil*, *Agnes' Eve*
And wonderful if flawed *Endymion*,
Glowed like golden clouds in his setting sun.
Death: and that very night the tears began
That welling from the Spanish Steps soon ran
All over mourning Europe to its end,
And down all time. There was no way to mend
That weeping wound in poetry's struck side;
History has wept more tears than can be dried.

There are great poems and great critics too:
They seldom meet, it's heaven when they do –
Though the usual match of course is flea-to-flea
And that's the little interest to me.

But sometimes I think of a man building a wall,
A big man setting little stones in place –
Or a little man with a presumptuous face
Who struts up cockily to a monolith
And thinks he'll put that in its place forthwith:
He strains and groans and all he does it for
Is a rupture and a mouthful of the moor.

Critics, beware the stone that will not budge!
Judgement is then a judgement of the judge,
Croker we know adjudged himself to hell;
We see his cloven hooves and arrowy tail . . .
But that's no use at all to dying Keats
Drowning in his sweat-wet bloodied sheets.

Hilary Corke

Judgement Lost

Much pious worship, where religion rules,
Prepares believers for their judgement day;
Such dreams of heaven, nature ridicules,
When all we have below is in decay.

We late arrivals on this ample Earth,
How shallow our assumption of command!
What is our depth of understanding worth?
What height of folly will the planet stand?

These human judgements are the ones that loom
Each modern measure tempting nature's power;
Increasingly we decorate our tomb
A plastic bloom replacing each wild flower.

Robert Marks

A Second Coming

Christ spat, they say, and caused the blind to see,
And people praised him for his miracles;
I try the same, and they spit back at me
Scorning my psalms and artless canticles.
I have no skill to fashion parables,
No seraphim to sing in my defence,
Only the myrrh of my experience . . .

There was a time I thought Jerusalem
A minute's walk away, a donkey ride.
Wearing the crumpled clothes of Bethlehem
I breathe hosannas. Now I have to hide
From those who walked with me; now I confide
Anxieties to men who fall asleep,
Or make complaint the message is too deep.

As to the judgement, what am I to say?
They hear my name and look for evidence
Of mediocrity; they push away
Signs of my strength as quaint coincidence.
Should I defend, with common arrogance,
The lines beneath the lines they would not see,
Or damn myself with mute humility?

Oh, I had second thoughts in moments, too,
Saw just a man who sang one simple song;
And serpent doubt invited me to view
A wiser world where judges don't belong.
A tempting voice insisted I was wrong
To sacrifice obscurity for shame,
To have my clothes stripped off, and call it fame.

But those who judged my works as second rate
Conferred a crown more exquisite than gold;
The lines I spoke are on the lips of fate
And time will tell how wisely I foretold.
It may well be that when the flesh is cold
And judges resurrect the words they read,
I'll have a second chance to raise the dead.

Frank McDonald

No Perfect Judge

When Jesus said to men with stones to cast
Let him who has no sin be first to throw,
He postulated no man should be classed
As fit to judge his fellows. Even so,

For civil life to prosper there's a need
For law and guardians of the law must be
Prepared to sentence those who fail to heed
The rules that govern their society.

In every generation, every land,
Where men would live with other men in peace,
There must be certain edicts that demand
Obedience to them, lest all order cease.

How choose, then, judges? Men with minds to weigh
The pros and cons of factual evidence;
Who know the law; the price it's right to pay
For breaking it; the victim's recompense

And other detail that the legal mind
Can master and make fair pronouncement on.
Such qualities as these we look to find
In those appointed. Who agree to don

The garb of justice, it is better they
Forget their own shortcomings when they act
In such capacity, since day to day
They judge of men whose guilt is proved by fact.

The tortured soul, too conscious that he might,
In other circumstance of fortune's plan,
Have found himself in the delinquent's plight,
Makes poorer judge although a better man.

Men of compassion, Christlike, wish that none
Need pay the direr penalties of crime.
So, that a gentler penal code be won,
Have changed men's sentencing from time to time.

Yet it remains that less than saintly men
Must judge of those who fall too far from grace.
That so, to pose the question asked again:
How choose we judges from the human race?

From earthly imperfections forced to choose,
None sinless, we must lesser sinners use.

Griselda Scott

Judges and Judging

He spoke in most judicious tone:
I'd own the words were not his own.
His robes were scarlet, wig was new —
And yet his words were quite askew.
Throughout, he radiated charm,
But filled the ears with sheer alarm.
Such careful phrasing, measured pace! —
A perfect case of pure disgrace.
He turned his honest eyes on me
And in them sat hypocrisy.
The sentence? Steady as a rock.
(They led me guiltless from the dock).

Susie Frail

Parting

Parting

When I left home – really left home, I mean –
My father saw me to the station. There,
Passive beside the cigarette machine,
We shuffled phrases through the smutted air.

'You're sure you've everything you want?' 'Yes, quite;
I don't need much for now.' 'I'll send the rest.'
'You needn't wait, you know.' 'It's quite all right.'
And then the train. 'Right ho, then. All the best.'

He strode off through the smoke for home, where he,
I later learned, broke down in tears. While I,
Speeding across the furrows, blinked to see
The unaccustomed brightness of the sky.

Noel Petty

Parting

See, lonely and clear against the winter night
The cold North Star and think of me.
But – I forgot! – there different stars shine bright:
The homely Southern Cross is what you'll see.

It won't be winter there. The sun will lay
Gold shadows on the southern sea
And warm the forest birds to sleep each day,
So hear their drowsy calls and think of me

Alone and empty in the London rain
For six long months, until we meet again.

Syrie Marx

Finale

In the spring of our ambition
When our innocence could pray,
And the serpent of derision
Had not lured our hearts away;
When our wishing was fulfilment
And fulfilment was our goal,
We were happy little buggers
But ambition took its toll.

In the summer of rejection
When we journeyed down to hell,
We were strangers to affection
And we bade success farewell.
Like Achilles we sat huffing
Feeling sore and getting pissed,
But the war went on without us
And we weren't even missed.

In our autumn of frustration
When no deity appeared
To enlighten contemplation
And disprove the things we feared,
We were angry little nothings,
We were literary fools,
And our only hope of heaven
Was to win the bloody pools.

Oh, but winter came upon us
Bringing laughter with the snow,
And we caught a glimpse of genius
Just as we were set to go.
Now fate emptied out its pockets
To supply the reasons why,
But as soon as we received them
It was time to say goodbye.

Frank McDonald

The Farewell Presentation

One clock stops. Tomorrow's hours
Float idle, washing with the tide;
Break upon nothing. Today's powers –
Office, position – set aside

After the formal stiff farewells,
The final clichés gravely meant;
The new clock's careful tick dispels
A lifetime's labouring, decades spent

Counting off days and measuring weeks:
The clock's inscription details dates.
A senior colleague lightly speaks
Of value, service; orchestrates

Hear hears, approval's murmuring drawls;
Quips briefly of the past, aware
Present engagements' pressing calls
Will him away. And so, elsewhere

Continuing, gritty hours run on,
The goodbyes' fading tones withdraw;
Familiar faces, smiles, are gone.
Only new-minted hours claw

Across your strange clock's brassy face
With hands as sharp as splintered glass.
Retirement's fractured fingers trace
The signposts pointing out to grass.

Tomorrow is another day,
Unshaped, disordered, with the first
Sour realisation of decay:
Each goodbye is a death rehearsed.

D. A. Prince

Kindertransport

Josef loves trains. He cannot wait to leave.
He asks about the sea. 'Will it be blue?
Is England far? Who will look after us?
And why is it that Mama can't come too?'

My mother says the steam is in her eyes
And that is why she cannot help the tears.
'Look after Josef. Be polite and good.'
The words crack open, shatter in my ears.

'How long', asks Josef, 'will the journey last?'
I should have used my eyes with greater care,
Remembered all the small things from my life.
My mother's fading, shrinking . . . 'soon be there . . .'

Adèle Geras

Say Goodbye to My Daughter

'Say goodbye to my daughter'
The frail old lady said.
Sitting and rocking quietly
In the chair beside her bed.

Her faded eyes were pleading
Tired hands plucked her shawl.
The ageing body trembled,
She heard someone in the hall.

'Say goodbye to my daughter'
Her voice was high and shrill.
'She's sure to be here shortly,
They told her I've been ill.'

I put my hand upon hers,
She gave a big blank stare.
Then looked far beyond me,
Still rocking in her chair.

'Say goodbye to my daughter . . .'
The plaintive voice went on.
And I, her only daughter,
Sat quiet 'til she was gone.

Elsie Mills

On Reading the Last Utterances of the Famous

When I am called upon to face
Expiry of my earthly lease,
I hope that I shall find the grace
To quit in dignity and peace,
To make my last farewells and go —
Like Tennyson or Socrates —
And from all I love and know
Still vocal, witty, and at ease,

But alas, I fear that I,
Confused, distressed, perhaps in pain,
Will find I cannot choose to die
In that well-bred, heroic vein,
Felicities of prose and rhyme
May not illumine my eclipse,
Indeed I'm sure that no sublime
Or gnomic truths will pass my lips,
Far more likely I'll expire
In silences of dark despair,
Or mouthing commonplaces dire
To cold unsympathetic air.

Philip A. Nicholson

Parting

Platforms are for parting. No figures float
So bleakly in the mind
As solitary ghosts on silent platforms,
Who gaze at one who's long since scorched away
To ransack art, or truth, or humankind.

All partings are an emblem of the end,
All nurse the traitor's kiss.
No matter if they trumpet doom or fate
Or rate no more than cinders in a grate,
All partings meet in this.

Roaring off to life, how could you know
My lowered eyes blurred.
Through all the paltry bric-à-brac of pain
I babbled on to halt the heaving train –
But I do not think you heard.

John Fairfax

The New Decade

Naivety Triumphant

Once more with jaundiced eyes
And countenance glum,
The cynics and the worldly-wise
Survey the year to come,

But like a child who runs to greet
The postman at the door
Or finds his hidden birthday treat
Within a secret drawer,

I can hardly wait to find
Those gifts to be revealed
When nineteen-ninety lifts the blind
On secrets long concealed,

For I know, with childish trust
That this will be the year
That smiles upon the truly just
And chills the rest with fear,

A time to breach the prison wall,
To free the fettered slave
To bring about the tyrant's fall
And dig the despot's grave,

A year in which the misanthrope
Defers to fools like me,
Who dare to dream and think and hope
Of better worlds to be.

Philip A. Nicholson

Sunlover's Salute to the Nineties

As festivities and jollities begin,
With a Euro voice we'll call the decade in,
We'll be done with being clannish,
Insularity will vanish,
And the Portuguese and Spanish
Will be kin.

We will sail to meet our cousins on the Rhine,
On the Danube we'll say *danke* for the wine,
And although it might be vulgar,
Drinking vodka on the Volga,
Perestroika-ing with Olga
Will be fine.

We'll have fun with basic French upon the Seine,
Making existential quips on auntie's pen,
We will nod our *obregadas*
On the Douro and the Tagus,
Cantaremos en bodegas
Down in Spain.

Goede morgen, we are *dronken* in the Hague,
British lions with the habits of a pig,
With our Dirty *Sun* beside us
There's no Kraut who will deride us
Do we care how Froggies chide us?
Not a fig!

We will welcome in the nineties, ring the bell
To let tourists know that they can come as well,
Just providing they have broghta
Load of money (as they oughta);
Will we clean our filthy water?
Will we hell!

Frank McDonald

A Day's March Nearer Home

To welcome Nineteen Ninety: let me think.
Will it be different from Eighty-Nine?
The sun will rise each day and, later, sink;
Some mornings wet and other mornings fine,

While all the news – the Media news I mean –
Will be of strife, catastrophe and such
But mostly pass me by. It's lately been
That way, since nothing ever changes much

In later years. Give me my thimbleful
That I may drink, not to myself but you,
In seemly manner. As I take my pull
I toast the ones who'll see the decade through.

A decade only, not a century?
It's hard to count the decades I have known.
Each one seemed briefer than the last to me
Although its steps grew slower with my own.

Yet, hope is mine. I wait without alarm
For the pressing invitation all receive
That could entice with the Pied Piper's charm
Should Nineteen Ninety be my year to leave.

Griselda Scott

The New Nineties

America harmonised its 'Gay Nineties' with barbershop
Quartets. The drums and clarinets of Sousa Bandsmen played
'The Stars and Stripes'. Flags waved. It seemed the music could not
    stop.
For crooning tenderfoots in love, it was a sweet decade.

In Berlin as the Bismarck Ball progressed, one guest remarked,
'Two Emperors, but a single waltz.' A swirling masquerade
Without an end. Men danced. 'Blue Danubes' wafted through the
    dark.
For Reichs embarking on the Rhine, there came a ripe decade.

In Paris at the Moulin Rouge, an Offenbach coquette
Might kick away her crimson frills in petticoat cascades
All night. What's she to lose? An image in the absinthe of Lautrec.
For *Folies* that dissolved in paint, he daubed a bright decade.

In Britain now the tunes have changed and Mrs Thatcher longs
To have the 'Nineties' back. She thinks them prim, Victorian,
And grim. She's wrong. The innocence of love is born in song.
This last decade of two millennia might sing along
To simple, sweeter, greener tunes. But then, I'm no historian.

K. Lloyd-Thompson

Valentines

Valentine for a Commuter

I see you every morning, bright and early:
The 8.15 provides my daily feast.
I only know you come from south of Purley
And at Victoria travel farther east.
I've watched you progress from the Fashion Pages
To City and Financial year by year;
Your simple frocks have changed in easy stages
To something more excitingly severe.
Could you permit the small chap with the pallor
At very least, to do your income tax?
The thought of what might follow gives me valour
To slip this card inside your filofax.
O dark enchantress of the District Line,
Will you consent to be my Valentine?

Noel Petty

To My Love

They all said hearts and flowers would do
To woo the one I long to woo.
My daisies wilted on the way;
The butcher's closed – it's his half day.

I think I've got it wrong again
And so I'll leave it to my pen
To form the words to tell you true
The only one I love is you.

Astrid Bartlett

To the Man in the Next Bedroom

Last night as I was missing you
I somehow came to blame
Rows of books on deadwood shelves,
A mug that bears your name,
Two hundred stencilled roses
An ancient coffee stain,
A moody piece of Dartmoor
Restrained in a metal frame.

While these things lay between us
As you sleep beyond the wall
How could I blame the little one
To whom I am in thrall?
Who's caused this separation,
Who's made suckers of us all,
Thanks to whom I've lost my figure
And a season at the ball.

This morning as the birds tuned up
I stumbled into bed
With lullaby throat and breastfeeder's back
And moondust in my head.
I thought of how I love you,
A phrase too often said,
And cursed my insufficient means
To show it to you instead.

This little lad that sleeps by me
Would not mean half so much
If he didn't have your silly smile,
Your sticky-out ears and such,
And I can sense your precious fingers
In his strong determined clutch,
And sweetheart I still yearn for you,
Your feel, your smell, your touch.

Janet Grunewald

Valentine

We of the Ladies' Luncheon Club
Who wear our hearts on cheque-book stub,
Because we're Tory through and through
Devotedly will vote for you.
Tired of familiar lacquered hair,
Of steely gaze and tones of care,
We long to run our fingers through
Your boyish locks, then look into
Those eyes whose colour is so right
And feel that handclasp warm and tight.
We tremble when we hear your name
That sets once-frigid hearts aflame;
We need a man of wholesome charms
Since erudition just alarms
The faithful at the sale or fête
Who like their speaker pretty wet.
Now as your star begins to shine
We'll raise more funds through Cheese and Wine;
Then will you be our Valentine,
Dear, tasteful Michael Heseltine?

Alanna Blake

A Valentine

When I was young and foolish
I heard a wise man say,
'Marry me! Marry me! Marry me!'
But lightly I said 'Nay'.

When I was young and lonely
A letter he did pen,
'Would God that you could love me!'
I laughed and said 'Amen'.

A ring upon my finger
It seemed a pretty token.
I thought a promise lightly made
As lightly could be broken.

Now care and time and children
Have bound me to his side;
And he has a loving wife,
Who had a thoughtless bride.

Did he with man's low cunning
Beguile me to be true?
Or was that thoughtless foolish girl
Yet wiser than she knew?

Mary Rae Campbell

Small Ads – Warm Heart

They advertised your presence in Provence
I phoned forthwith, a headlong rush of hope
A week with Wendy in the South of France
A promise to put Heaven in a trance
Or suscitate a hermit to elope
They advertised your presence in Provence.

Though christened James not Galahad or Lance
Susceptible but resolute to cope
A week with Wendy in the South of France
A call to arms, a signal to advance
To liberate a latent misanthrope
They advertised your presence in Provence.

Wry lampoonist of laureates enhance
My Valentine and grapple where I grope
A week with Wendy in the South of France
At Arles we'll dine, at Avignon we'll dance
And cogitate what Porter owes to Pope
They advertised your presence in Provence.

I'd stride the Cevennes shoeless for a glance
From one whose rhyme and sense defines her scope
A week with Wendy in the South of France
Has been rescinded – not the slightest chance!
Must Dannie Abse see me sob and mope?
They advertised your presence in Provence
A week with Wendy in the South of France.

Jim Smith

Dear Miss Plover

Oh Emily, your pale remembered thighs
Come back to haunt me now in Kensal Rise,
Your lips, your arms, your breasts that draw the eyes
And, wobbling under cover, tantalise;
Me wretched here and you superb in Bonn,
Such charms by lowly clerks are rarely won.

The amorous festival is drawing near
But you're in Germany and I am here,
Reply to this my blond, seconded fair
And I will meet you coming through the air;
I'll travel on an airplane or a sigh
Your humble EO in the DTI.

I have no home or capital to give
The life is mean the two of us should live,
This is parochial love I offer you
No European vistas will we view,
The dog, the wireless and China tea.

Send me a *coup de fil* before I die
All-conquering virgin speak, and let me fly.

Austin Johnson

91

Valentine

I thought I saw a softness in your eye
Last night as we were making Christmas plans
It seems the moment's come when even I
Must bare a heart like any other man's.
You make me laugh; when you pronounce my name
It doesn't sound so humdrum after all;
I feel so easy with you, all the same
I don't believe your company could pall.
It's not your beauty only, beauty fades,
Integrity? perhaps, and something more
A nameless quality in you persuades
Me you're the perfect one I've waited for.
I'm serious for once, so darling say
You love me too and we can choose a day.

Ginger Jelinek

The Birth of Twins

A Schoolmaster's Lament

Have I dreamed, perhaps, an improbable dream,
Or hoped an unlikely hope?
For the fruits of my yearning have not been seen,
And I rail at the Fates, and mope:

'Oh where are the children of whom one hears,
The wise ones, the clever, the pretty?
Those who remember to scrub out their ears,
Who occasionally say something witty?

'Oh where are the well-born whose mothers drink gin,
Who listen to Tallis and Verdi?
Have they all been locked up in some tiresome bin
Full of lunatick doctors and clergy?

'I think that they must, for I never see them.
Those whom I teach cannot spell.
And they're all frightfully loud, and so frightfully heathen,
And some of them actually smell.

'So there's no hope for me; there's no hope.
My dreams are shattered like glass.
My lot, it would seem, lies among the obscene:
The sprigs of the philistine class.'

But what is that vile, distant bawling?
What are those bundles that hiss,
That cling to those dugs, those domes quite appalling,
And shower the midwife in piss?

The nurse answers, 'Twins are upon us!'
The fair one's called Hope, it appears.
The darker is known as Experience.
'Oh aren't they a couple of dears!'

'Children?' I ask, somewhat startled;
'My girl, can you really be sure?
For I've never seen any who're that small before,
Or such delicate, saffron manure.'

The babies fall suddenly silent,
While the midwife dries herself off.
Experience leers with a look slightly violent;
Hope essays a small cough.

'Have I dreamed an improbable dream?' I muse,
'Or hoped an unlikely hope?
If the fruits of my yearning never were seen,
I'd hang up my head with a rope.'

So I reach for a gin, and some Tallis,
And thus suitably armed, I elope
Whither these twins are ever upon us:
Eternal Experience and Hope.

Wealands Bell

Inspiration's Gemination

The dark twin offers disillusioned sighs,
The bitterness of age's empty well,
The acid taste that makes us realise
Our modest minds have nothing much to sell.
His gloomy whisper shatters the belief
That toil can somehow compensate for skill;
Our poor possessions lure no passing thief,
Our labour yields no fruit, and never will.

The bright twin pours a glass and we sit back
Content with our contentment, pleased to be
Part of life's hazy, boozy almanac,
Laughing with friends in jesting company.

We've buried God in brilliant, bubbling wine
And blown away his creeds with fat cigars,
We're guttersnipes with Oscar as we dine,
And sure as hell we're looking at the stars.

The dark twin finds us clearing up the mess,
Our years are empty bottles, thrown away
With dismal smash; the sound of our success
Was just the popping corks of yesterday.
We know, we know, he has no need to speak,
Our grandeur is the rubble of the least,
We raise the bucket-lid, compliant, meek,
And brush away the fragments of a feast.

Then come the moments when the fingertips
Grasp at some truth, a nuance we ignored,
And once again there's laughter on our lips,
As we discover lands, still unexplored.
Strange how they tease us, drive us through despair,
Then wipe away the stains of our regret,
Strange how they grant a poetaster's prayer,
And let him think there's poetry in him yet.

Frank McDonald

Star Maps

See Leto running through the starry night,
Chased by the mad Queen's serpent. What a way
To end her pregnancy! What price to pay
For one ecstatic moment of delight,
Coupling like sparrows in their nuptial flight.

At last, in Delos, by a date-palm tree
Her travails end: With a triumphant cry,
The Twins rise, glinting through the evening sky.
The stars wait imperturbably to see
Such brave addition to their company.

And what of Leto? She'll have no redress.
With figure ruined, reputation gone,
She'll never make it to the Parthenon.
Perhaps she'll make a fortune and confess
('The quail who loved me') to the Sunday Press.

I see them, painted on my astral globe:
Leto, the serpent striking at her robe,
Hera, obsessed with frantic jealous eye,
The Twins in lucent aristocracy,
All frozen in contention – save for Zeus
Who's off on other amorous pursuits.

B. Kaye

The Birth of Twins

Just as her trolley parts the doors
Big Sophie from Barbados roars
'Now slow down it' not a race'
And – 'Hello girls – you save' my place?'
Our fav'rite patient takes the floor,
We can't believe she's back for more.

'Now is you nurses keepin' count?
On how dem little beggars mount,
Mi folks be thinkin' you's mi kin
Because 'arm always comin' in,
Lord be praised in highest heaven
'Arm to part wid number seven.'

Dear Sophie cries 'OH GLORY BE!'
I take her hand, she clings to me,
But soon is born a healthy boy
Big Sophie beams a mother's job,
But she's not finished – what is this?
A baby girl for added bliss.

Poor Sophie rolls her big brown eyes
'You nurse' is bad to tell me lies.
Oh Lordy, Lordy take one back
You all is bound to get the sack.
Just how come I be gettin' twins?
He only love' me once,' she grins.

Jenny Smith

Twins

Two spheres of cells cleft from a single egg
Hang silent in the vast cathedral womb.
From creeping puckered limb-bud grows a leg
And human form is woven on the loom.

With lidless eyes the brothers view the night
And in each other's arms held, feel dull sound,
And even now they know the link is tight
And none can break the love by which they're bound.

Beneath the striplights' mockery of day
Quick hands, cold sheathed, will cut and reach within.
Masked monsters, heedless, carry them away
And acts of caring violence begin.

Their birth, a new beginning or an end?
Triumphant entry to the world of man,
Or loss of all they've known and of a friend?
O sleeping sons-to-be, dream while you can.

Julius Welby

Foolishness

Biting the Hand

Dear Editor,
           You are a fool
To institute the petty rule
That puts an arbitrary ban
On verse that doesn't rhyme or scan!
Free verse, in good hands, can be taut,
Elliptical and finely-wrought;
Who knows what masterpieces are
Excluded by this foolish bar?
Four hundred pounds a month could be
A prize for *proper* poetry –
Not thrown away on lightweight lines
Like February's Valentines
Tossed off by refugee technicians
From certain other competitions.
I am a double fool, you say,
For thinking thus, and for the way
I follow slavishly that rule
I rail against. Not so! A fool
Is one who, confidently wise,
Knows not where his best interest lies.
We all have flaws – ah, yes indeed!
While yours is folly, mine is greed.

Peter Norman

The Foolish Virgins

The five wise virgins trimmed their lamps
And checked their flasks of oil;
Engaged in ladylike pursuits
They filled the hours with toil.

Five foolish virgins killed the time
With trivial, girlish chat,
Put too much make-up on, swapped jokes,
Giggled at this and that.

The five wise virgins lowered their eyes;
Demurely reticent
They waited for the groom's approach,
Counting the time well spent.

Five foolish virgins messed about,
Their clothes were cheap and tarty
It didn't match their smarter plans
To hang on for a party.

Their lamps burned out – they had no spares;
Each shrugged: it was a lark
To shriek imagined fears, and tell
Ghost stories in the dark.

The groom arrived, a little late
To start the nuptial ball;
He glanced at them and looked away.
They weren't his sort at all.

The five wise virgins followed him;
Each drank a small sweet sherry
And clutched her lamp, and told her friends
That this was awf'lly merry.

Five foolish virgins made rude signs
Then went off to a bar;
Fell in with younger, monied guys
Who stood them caviar.

They drank champagne and Armagnac;
Virginity was over.
Each caught a BMW-ed mate
And well-heeled life in clover.

Their servants clean electric lamps,
Their husbands meet the bills.
Five foolish matrons laugh and dance
In fish-net tights and frills.

The five wise virgins, dry old sticks,
Grow old and grim and grey;
Still ignorant of foolish fun
They genteelly decay.

D. A. Prince

Foolishness

It isn't so much that he dithers and dreams
It isn't the fact that he strays;
And nor is it simply the fact that he seems
To be living so much in a daze.

He goes with a friend to the Club for a drink,
Arranges to meet for a game,
At bedtime he's trying his hardest to think
Of the place and the date and the name.

He's often dishevelled but mainly because
He has chosen himself what to wear;
Shirts that are dredged from the bottom of drawers
And socks that are seldom a pair.

It isn't the fact that if he should go out
Whatever the mission might be,
He'll surely forget what the mission's about:
It's mainly the fact that he's me.

Ted Giles

Poet's Foolishness

When readers with intelligence
Are asked to rhyme and scan
And in the process make good sense
Of 'Foolishness' they can
But designate that 'poet' a fool
Poseur or charlatan
Who denigrates each classic rule
Of meaning, form and plan.

The ugly, stilted, jerky prose
The stumbling, halting line
The metaphors which juxtapose
The urine with the wine
Are tricks to shock but show as fools
Those 'poets' who won't define
Their thoughts with words, precision tools
To fashion a design.

Do 'poets' homes have ill-hung doors
Bricks laid without plumb-line
With bulging walls and buckled floors
Of green and warping pine?
To leaking taps and flushless loos
Do modern 'poets' incline?
Or choose but poetry to abuse
And mark their own decline?

For foolish 'poets' there is one cure
Which they should undergo
To polish meaning and ensure
Their pointless poems show
More sense and strength; they must review
Their habits and forego
Their *Waste Land* wanderings and eschew
A daily diet of *Crow*.

John Twells

God's Fool

I never sought a burning bush or sign
Written in God's own hand across a wall,
I never tasted blood instead of wine,
Nor lay awake for deities to call.
I yawned through paternosters, like a swine
I found no beauty in the pearls of Paul,
When priest or ayatollah called for prayer
I found no note that made me wish to hear.

Yet in my empty journeyings abroad
The things I see have no intrinsic worth,
I hear imperfect choirs, and applaud,
I bury love with sorrow in the earth;
Only a fool believes an infant god
Grew into manhood from some virgin birth,
Yet age would have me wander back to school,
Abandon wisdom and become a fool.

Is it a fear that Charon will arrive
And ask a pennyworth of faith from me?
Or just a wish that something may survive
To bless my thoughts with immortality?
To be God's fool and keep the soul alive
Seems such a paltry, undemanding fee;
Why then should earthly wisdom overrule
A coward's wish to be a faithful fool?

Frank McDonald

Foolishness

She sat at the Sainsbury's check-out.
The lights seemed to dance in her hair.
She smiled, and my heart started pumping,
And I could do nothing but stare.

She became my daily obsession.
Her smiles set my feelings on fire.
How I longed to make my confession
And tell of my love and desire.

But Cupid had kept it a secret.
My love, he intended to smother.
My heart missed a beat at the check-out
Her seat had been filled by another!

Then I heard a harsh voice in the background.
Said a girl, with a wink and a nod,
'That Pensioner fancied our Janice –
But he's harmless, the silly old sod!'

Now another girl sits at the check-out,
And I've fallen in love with her smile.
Being foolish can make life worth living,
And foolishness makes mine worth while!

Eric Rosser

Matthew 25:2

We met first at the County ground
That summer when the wickets
Were fast, and bowlers bounced balls high.
We'd bought adjacent tickets.

He sat beside me, flask in hand,
His sandwiches were cheese.
By close of play we knew both names
His Greg to my Louise.

The next weekend we met again
Some dinner then a play.
He brushed his hand against my thigh
I moved my leg away.

Next time together we held hands
His lips caressed my finger.
He wore a spicy aftershave,
He left . . . Its perfume lingered.

That night I lay in bed alone
Regretting his departure.
Next time he came, for sure he'd stay;
His presence flamed my ardour.

The chilled champagne has all been drunk
The candle light is dim.
My heart misses a beat, I lie
My body next to him.

The next weekend I stand below
The clock of the Town Hall.
Ten minutes late, it's unlike him
Perhaps he tried to call?

I sit and contemplate my loss
I'd needed little urging.
Here, wiser now, with some regret,
A foolish, now ex, virgin.

A. Meyrick

Foolishness

The way her lidded, languid eye
Gave mine a moment's glance
Across the teapot-studded room
I knew I had a chance.

And later, when we crossed upon
A path of broken shale,
Her almost smile, it seemed to say:
'Of course, you cannot fail.'

My friends were all of one accord,
To whit, I had her won.
'You're well in mate.' 'Don't mess about.'
'Get in there my old son.'

So finally I challenged her,
All confident and suave,
And told her if she turned me down
I'd pine, I'd waste, I'd starve.

She lifted that half-lidded eye,
Inclined her brow and said:
'Oh go away you stupid man.
On second thoughts, drop dead.'

Some men can fool you, women too,
Your eyes, the wind, the tide,
But none can do it quite so well
As vanity inside.

Joseph Houlihan

The Ideal of Womanliness

Commercials for Women

Ceres, Demeter, Nature, Mother Earth!
Offspring of blind *Economy* and *Worth*,
Goddess of Hygiene, handmaid of Fast Food,
Blithe Doormat to thy Lord and darling Brood,
O *MUM*, I sing – thine ancient temple floor
Neat-chequered black-and-white gleam evermore!
Thou paragon of Peace (whose only ill
Is swiftly staunched by effervescent Pill),
Long may thy Smile send out that signal Spark
Of teeth protected from pernicious Plaque!
Thy water-closet glistens, Woe betide
Known Germs that, reckless, venture there to hide!
Daily the lonely Huntress' path you tread,
Eager to snare the whitest-sliciest Bread,
Wisely eschewing common Market Stall
To sack the sumptuous Supermarket Hall
(Nor *Chop*, nor *Cheese*, thou know'est, is deep-down Clean
Unless thrice-wrapped in sealing *Polythene*).
Claim, Mum, as day declines, your just reward –
See the admiring Family applaud,
As on the Altar, spotlessly arrayed,
Your ozone-friendly Casserole is laid:
Greedy they gorge – 'tis loved by Everyone.
You smile. Who cares if they have left you None?
Behold her younger Sister. Tell it, Muse!
Sing of her low-cut dress and high-heeled Shoes:
Unfold her myst'ry, why she is adored,
Though never seen at Sink or Ironing Board;
Nor shops at Tesco, doesn't clean the Loo,
(And has poor Taste in Coffee, *entre nous*).
Yet men of every Class are ravished quite;
Turn into Trees, astonished at her sight;
Pursue her wafted Fragrance through the Street;
And feed her every Sort of candied Treat.

Tho' candy never shaped her waist, I vow;
Nor *Sol*, nor *Sorrow*, ever lined her brow,
(Save, for a moment, when by Passion led
She strews Spaghetti o'er a Serpent's head).
Nor does *Simplicity* her Beauty mar:
She'll wield a Briefcase, power-drive a Car.
A fan-belt snaps? She strips a stockinged thigh.
Designer-iguanas feast her eye.
In Bath or Boardroom, see her Nordic cool!
E'en caught shampooing in a Mountain Pool!
Age cannot wither her. Should wrinkles come,
She'll not end up, like Sister, playing MUM,
But ever haunt the Club, agog to know
The bitter-sweet ingredients of *Cointreau*.

Elusive Woman! Which of these is true?
Earth Mother? Harlot? Are there only two?

Colin Pearson

The Collapse of Communism

When Means Become the Ends

At first, ideals; and then the power
With marching feet to match the hour,
And nourish Revolution's might
To keep the flame forever bright.

Humanity is not enough;
The State, reliable and tough
Must be the Means, unceasingly,
To crush dissent and tame the free.

So State control became the End
To which each servile knee must bend.
The State was All; the State alone
Would shape the course and smoothy hone
Ideals for which they bravely fought,
And cherished goals so dearly bought.
Until with courage multiplied
A continent regained its pride.

Now Market Forces haunt our screens.
Shall Ends, once more, give way to Means?

John Bostock-Smith

Heat

There Was a Moment

There was a moment, brief as passing sin,
When I could feel the soft lips of the sun
Release each sense and every nerve unpin
Until my flesh, it seemed, was all new spun.
And from the tissue of my glowing skin,
Alive with sharp sensation, sweetest sense,
Stretched out a thousand tentacles to win
Some further joy from this heat, so intense.
But now those silky lips press cruelly down
And suck my soul up through my every pore
To leave the husk behind. My soul will drown
In those fair lips or else burn to the core.
And so foul whorish heat leads us all on
Through paths of pleasure till our soul is gone.

Diana Beharrell

Heat

They sat upon a mossy bank
His arm around her waist
No-one could doubt that they were there
The joys of love to taste.

The meadow green, the sky so blue!
They'd never been so sweet
With daisies and with buttercups
Both nestling round their feet.

Bliss! and rapture! Love's young dream
Was manifested there
Beside the coolly flowing stream
Where was no wordly care.

The future mattered not at all
The past was dead and gone.
As they embraced they were in thrall
With Earth they seemed as one.

And as the heat enveloped them
It was a warmth combined
With nature's plan – immutable –
For future humankind.

Elizabeth Borland

The Sea! The Sea!

Of Seas and Galleons

Sunset galleon, sunset galleon, moving through a dreamer's ocean
Let them label you illusion or an old man's foolish notion,
But the waves on which you shiver surely lead towards a heaven
To a seaside, to a childhood in which faults are all forgiven.

I can bleach your greying canvas, I can resurrect your timber,
I can raise your sunset standards like a phoenix from an ember,
And the beauty that I give you will lend purpose to my dreaming,
As I wander down to board you in the solace of my scheming.

In the soft September silence of my evening adoration
You are everything and nothing, like the whisper of creation,
On the skyline there are breakers, there are islets that surround you
As I let my fancies voyage to the ocean where I found you.

My awareness keeps you moving, and my faith prevents your sinking,
Your existence is as misty as the margin of my thinking,
And I wonder, for a moment, is it I who am the shadow,
Is my garden just the glimmer of a brighter, greater meadow?

Evening galleon, evening galleon I would sail with you for ever
If my heart could know the secrets of the cargoes you deliver,
I would sacrifice my winter for a promise to be driven
To the bay of some bright Eden, to the estuary of heaven.

Does the sea that I am watching, with its little flecks of foam,
Bear the whip marks of a Xerxes, or the broken oars of Rome?
Was it there that Homer pictured Agamemnon's fleet at Troy,
And did Virgil find Aeneas on such oceans in the sky?

Far beyond the dreamer's borders who can say what longships sail
With their Norsemen braving dragons on the very edge of hell?
Are there battles still continuing to which the world is blind
In the Actiums, Lepantos and Trafalgars of the mind?

Does it matter, will it matter that the ocean is unreal,
That the craft we thought could save us does not move, and never
    will?
Does it matter if an old man, tired of finding no replies,
Builds himself a perfect vessel from the substance of the skies?

Evening galleon, evening galleon soon your sea will be a mist,
And no dreamer in a garden will attest that you exist,
Soon the mind that made your moment, like a bank of rising spray,
Will be swallowed by time's ocean and like you be wiped away.

Frank McDonald

Anstruther Harbour: Notes for a Painting

From the lighthouse, when the view
Was clear, the hills of Edinburgh could
Be seen, the edges of the world I knew.
Pillars of Hercules, twin piers that stood
Between my childish world and adulthood.
Although the picture looks the same
The past is painted in a smaller frame.

There must have been rain then, but time
Has washed its muddy recollection clean.
I see a Sun, which seemed to shine
All summer long. My memory has been,
No doubt, impaired, or blinded by the beams.
The flash-backs burn me as they pass
The past is better seen through darkened glass.

I speak of years, of distant dates
For now the town is squeezed by sea and sky
Into a line which separates
The deep from deep. Although I learned to fly
And swim some time ago, yet often I
Return, a native now bereft
To recollect something I might have left.

The water sparkles, but the light
Is temporary, it forgets my name.
Yet I can walk the rocks at night
Blindfolded; all the paths are still the same
They know my footsteps, know the way I came.
Time between ebbs like the tide
I paint myself a corner here to hide.

I step into the picture, meet
Myself; I fish, I swim, I once lived here.
The paint dries hard and plastic, yet
Through it I scent the salt wind off the pier.
The smell of seaweed lingers through the years
Here I am twelve, here nine, here three
Where every walking ghost I meet is me.

I saw a dolphin gambol here
I see her leaping still, blue-black and grey
The acrobat below the pier
The light refracting rainbows in her spray.
Her time is gone, and time can not repay
The loss, the prism in the rain,
I do not think that she will rise again.

The sea anemone will close
Its petal on the land. It flowers best
Where it was born, as does the rose.
Water, wind and waves beat in my breast
They are enough for me; much of the rest
Is tricks. Who wants to dine with kings?
I want to lie here where the mermaid sings.

My father traced his father's line
Towards the winter herring. I was first
To chart a passage that was mine.
And yet, I feel, my voyage was accursed;
The ocean is too small to quench my thirst
For home, for haven. Though I journey far
This harbour light is still my guiding star.

C. Jack

Index of Poets

Index of Titles and First Lines